HIDDEN HISTORY *of* AMELIA ISLAND

HIDDEN HISTORY *of* AMELIA ISLAND

Jeff Suwak

Published by The History Press
Charleston, SC
www.historypress.com

Front cover: Vintage photograph of American Beach. *Image from A.L. Lewis Museum at American Beach, https://allewismuseum.org/. Used with permission.*
Back cover: Vintage postcard of woman on Fernandina Beach looking at buried treasure. *Image from the Amelia Island Museum of History, https://ameliamuseum.org/.*

First published 2024

Manufactured in the United States

ISBN 9781467155779

Library of Congress Control Number: 2023950470

Notice: The information in this book is true and complete to the best of our knowledge. It is offered without guarantee on the part of the author or The History Press. The author and The History Press disclaim all liability in connection with the use of this book.

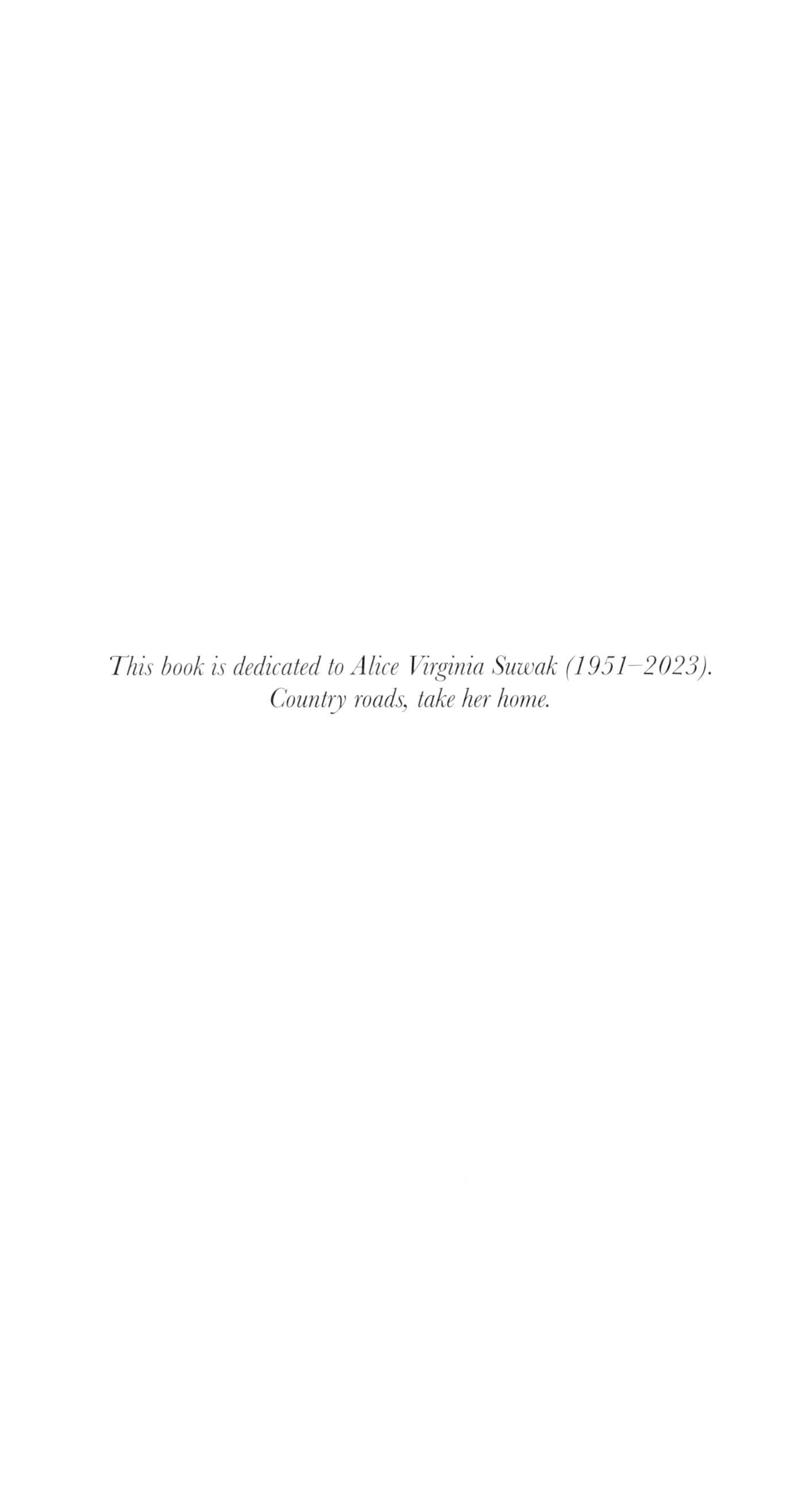

This book is dedicated to Alice Virginia Suwak (1951–2023).
Country roads, take her home.

Contents

1. The Adventure Begins 13
The Man Who Talked to Rattlesnakes and Alligators 14
Widely Loved and Little Known 16
Rattling Ghost Chains 17
Lay of the Land 18

2. Castaways, Shipwrecks and Buried Treasure 19
The Gold Beneath the Sand 19
Phantom Trees and Ghost Chains 20
The Expedition of T. Howard Kelly 21
Amelia Island Treasures Found Through the Years 22
Aury's Gold 23
The San Miguel*: A Ship Beneath the Waves* 24
A Philadelphia Quaker in King Charles II's Spanish Mission 26

3. An Island by Any Other Name 28
Lovelorn Princess Amelia 28
The Man Who Named It 30
And It Shall Be Called Fernandina 30
Napoyca 30

4. Napoyca: Before European Eyes 31
An Old, Old People 33
Timucuan Pottery 33

5. Embargo This: Amelia Becomes a Dark Port 36

6. Murderers, Marauders and Pirates 38
The Captain, the Pirate and the Governor's Son 38
Harmon Murray 40
The Killing of Deputy Jeremiah "Jerry" Mattox 43
Enter Jim Coe, Cold Case Detective 43
The Assassination of Dr. Elisha Graham Johnson 45
Jacksonville Mutiny and the Firing Squad at Fort Clinch 46
What Does This All Mean? 48
Mansion House and the Murder of F.C. Suhrer 48
Like So Many Rats: Amelia Island Shipwrecks 50
Anonymous and Torn in Two 50
The Olivette 50
Met Death Calmly and Died Easy: Merrick Jackson's Execution 51

7. Hoist, Lower, Hoist—Repeat: The Story of Amelia's Eight Flags 53
Jean Ribault, French Florida and the Isle of May, 1562–64 53
Ribault Before Florida 54
The Isle of May 55
Among Them Were Gentlemen: Rene Goulaine de Laudonnière and Bloody Fort Caroline 57
Massacre at Matanzas 58
French Vengeance 60
Forged in Blood: First Spanish Amelia 62
Santa Maria, Spanish Amelia 62
The Sun Sets on the First Spanish Amelia 65
An Amelia Island Affair for the Ages: The Ballad of Gregor MacGregor 66
MacGregor Before Amelia 66
An Amelia Island Affair for the Ages 67
George Clarke and Fernandina Rebuilt Anew 70
Battle of Amelia Island 73
McClure's Hill 74
French-Mexican Revolutionary Louis Aury 75
Aury at Amelia 76
Aury's Defeat 78
Amelia Under Britain 80

Governor James Moore and the English Attack 80
We Are the Egmont Isle, Coo Coo Ca Choo 82
A Gray Season 82
James Oglethorpe: Best Damn Squatter in U.S. History 83
Egan's Indigo 85
The Night They Burned Ol' Fernandina Down 86
1794: Une Parenthèse à la Française (A French Interlude) 87
Patriot War of East Florida 88
Revolutionary War Amelia 90
Confederate Swan Song 91
The Train That Exploded 92
Dupont Cometh 93
Yulee's Dream: The Florida Railroad 93
Amelia Island, United States of America 94

8. Chloe Merrick and the Civil War Orphanage That Was a Mansion 95
Merrick in Fernandina 95
Finegan's House 97

9. Extra! Extra! The First Newspaper on Amelia Island 99

10. American Beach: Recreation and Relaxation Without Humiliation 101
Abraham Lincoln Lewis 102
The Beach Lady 104
NaNa Dune 107
Evans's Rendezvous 108
The Streets of American Beach 110
Franklintown 111
Franklintown United Methodist Church 111

11. Amelia Forts 113
Fort San Carlos 113
Fort Clinch 114

12. Plantations 115
Harrison Plantation and Harrison Family Cemetery 115
Yellow Bluff Plantation and the Fernandez Preserve 116

13. Amelia Changes the Modern Shrimping Industry 117
T.E. Fischer 117
A New Way to Shrimp 118
Amelia's Master Boatbuilder 121
Amelia's Master Net Makers 122

14. About Town 123
Bosque Bello: The Beautiful Forest Where Fernandina's Dead Speak 123
Old Town Fernandina, Where the Streets Have Moved 124
Probably the First Inn on Fernandina Beach 124
Golden Age of Amelia Island (1869–1915) 125
Hard Times, County Seat Fernandina 126
The Yellow Fever of 1877 127
Florida House Inn 128
Amelia Island Light 129
Centre Street Post Office 131
Old Nassau County Courthouse 131
Lesesne House 132
Captain Bell's Pippi Longstocking House 134
Robert Sands Schuyler, Architect 134
Tabby House 135
Fairbanks House 135
The Amelia Schoolhouse Inn 135
St. Peter's Episcopal Church 136
Frank Lloyd Wright and the Blue Herron Inn 136

15. Florida Cash and Fernandina's First Newspaper 137

16. Each of Us Must Play a Part: The People of Fernandina 138
Mary Mattair, Who Raised a Family in the Wilderness 138
Felipa the Witch 139
The Sisters of Saint Joseph 140
Mayor Charles Albert 141
Amos Latham: The First Lighthouse Keeper 141

17. Gilberto Shrimping Weed Boat of 1977 143
DIAMANTE 145
Sorry for the Weight 146

18. Just A-Passing Through: Stories of Amelia's
Notable Visitors 147
Zora Neale Hurston Married in Fernandina 147
Harriet Tubman in Fernandina 147
Bandit McGirt 148

Bibliography 151
About the Author 155

Chapter 1

The Adventure Begins

Welcome to fabulous Amelia Island!

It's also been called Napoyca, Île de Mai, Isla de Santa María and the Isle of Eight Flags. Each name holds a story, and there are many, many other tales besides.

Beneath the island's cobblestones and sands lies a richness of history entirely disproportionate to its physical size (which is roughly equivalent to New York's Manhattan Island). Amelia's bones are composed of pirate treasure literal and metaphorical, shards of ancient pottery, slave chains broken and tossed aside, astounding tales of bravery, scenes of savagery and a polite dash of madness (well, maybe more than a polite dash).

Amelia has been the stage for terrible follies and fantastic triumphs that still hold the power to inspire centuries after their occurrence. It's loved today for its mellow vibe, quaint downtown and beautiful beaches, but blood has been spilled on these sands. Buried here are the crooked skeletons of men and women who endured severe physical hardship to transform the island into a home.

Eight different flags have flown over Amelia. Some, such as the Spanish and English flags, are recognizable today. Others, such as the Green Cross of Gregor MacGregor and the Patriot Flag of General George Mathews, were tossed aside as quickly as they were hoisted.

Meanwhile, figures such as Abrahan Lincoln Lewis and Solicito "Mike" Salvador helped make Amelia a cultural and commercial landmark. All those stories are told in the tome currently in your hands.

Vintage postcard showing Camp Amelia, Fernandina, Florida, 1898. *Amelia Island Museum of History.*

The island owes the richness of its story to multiple variables, but in particular to two peculiarities. First, Amelia possesses one of the deepest natural channels on the Eastern Seaboard. Second, its geographic position made it a strategic nexus between world powers and the common people traveling between them.

In this book, you'll learn about Amelia's many twists and turns, heroes and villains, victories and defeats. An intriguing cast of characters befitting a Charles Dickens novel awaits.

So with that, friends, let's get digging.

The Man Who Talked to Rattlesnakes and Alligators

Amelia Island, 1900. An old man stirs to the sound of rattling chains. He raises his head, peers out the window of his palmetto-thatched hut, sees in his backyard a live oak with a chain hanging from its branch and mysteriously swinging on a still night, smiles at the unseen ghost playing its old, doomed part… He smiles, lies back down, and sleeps…

Kings and queens have played their parts on Amelia Island. So, too, have brigands and businessmen, pirates, captains and crooks. Yet our story starts with a different kind of character.

Image from a newspaper article about "Jimmie" Drummond (it misspells "Jimmy"). Belleville Daily Advocate, *November 22, 1928.*

"Uncle" Jimmy Drummond left his mark through sheer originality and personality. Born without fancy titles or resources, he nevertheless lived a fascinating life that influenced the people around him.

Drummond starts our tale because he makes the perfect tour guide for an exploration of the hidden history of Amelia. He embodied the mystery and magic of the island.

There are the facts of history, and there are facts of the imagination. In a mystical place like Amelia Island, it's often hard to tell the difference between the two. And would we want it any other way? We're here for history, yes, but also for mystery—the poetry of the past.

Uncle Jimmy Drummond shows us the way.

Widely Loved and Little Known

Drummond liked to tell people he was a full-blooded Seminole Indian, though many questioned that claim. It's been suspected that he was full-blooded African American or both Seminole and African. Either way, no one cared too much, because Drummond lived outside the bounds of normal reality, and that's why people loved him.

In an era long before YouTube or cable television, Drummond became a grassroots celebrity though force of personality alone. He was unusual and amusing—a great storyteller. A June 2, 1933 edition of the *Nassau County Leader* reported that hundreds of people from throughout the United States "made frequent trips to the Island to pay the old Seminole a visit and hear tales of his escapades."

Drummond kept rattlesnakes in a pen in his bedroom. Rumors abounded that the snakes came to his call like dogs. One witness to the phenomenon was a physician named Humphrey, who went to Drummond's home because Drummond didn't like going to doctors. According to lore, the doctor asked Jimmy about the claims that he could talk to snakes.

As recounted in *Stories from Bosque Bello*, Drummond, in response, made a "curious sound," and a huge rattlesnake slithered into the room. His self-preservation winning out over curiosity, Humphrey high-tailed it out of there. One imagines Drummond smirking to himself as the doctor fled.

Drummond was believed to practice folk magic. We don't know if it was hoodoo, something tied to Seminole spirituality or something else entirely. Whatever the school of magic was, his sorcerous ways appear to have been the object of fascination rather than fear.

Jimmy lived north of Atlantic Avenue, close to the modern entrance to Fort Clinch. Stories abounded that he survived mostly by foraging and hunting, which wouldn't have been inconceivable. The waters were full of abundant food then. A person could toss a seine net into the water and watch fish fill it within minutes.

Drummond pops up in Amelia history in unexpected ways and places. In one *Fernandina Observer* story about survivors of the hurricane of 1898, Drummond is revealed to have sheltered the Baker family during the storm.

An article circulating around national newspapers in October 1928 described Drummond visiting the grave of Father Pedro Martínez, a Catholic martyr killed while doing missionary work in Florida. Drummond said his grandfather first took him to the grave and told him the story of the murder, adding that "the good father did not die in vain, and his slayers were duly punished for the murder" (according to the October 2, 1928 *Seminole Morning News*). Drummond looked forward to meeting the martyr himself in the afterlife.

The paper closes with a verbal snapshot of Drummond from back in a time when journalists were allowed to be poetic now and then: "Often the aged 'Uncle Jimmie' will find transportation to the grave, for he is too feeble now to walk, and sit for hours muttering a weird jargon of another day and crooning a melody of reverence."

Some sources mention that Drummond worked at Amelia Island Light for forty years. He's not on record as ever having been a lightkeeper, but there are other jobs he might have been doing, so it's possible. Drummond claimed that he served on a Union warship named the USS *Pawnee*. Black sailors did serve on that ship, so it's possible that Drummond jumped on while the *Pawnee* made a confirmed stop in Fernandina, but records suggest he more likely would have served on the USS *Perry*, if he did indeed serve at all (no military records have been found to validate his claims).

In 1933, Drummond passed away from diphtheria. He was believed to be 107 years old.

Full Seminole? Part Seminole? Who knows, and who cares? He was all Uncle Jimmy Drummond, and he will be our guide through our tour of the hidden history of Amelia Island.

ENCOUNTER WITH RATTLER.

Florida Boy on Bicycle Attacked by Monster Reptile.

FERNANDINA, Fla., Sept. 2.—One of the most thrilling affairs in the way of a snake experience happened to a young son of C. B. Royal, an employe of the Seaboard Air Line railway at Yulee.

It appears the young fellow, who is only about 12 or 13 years old, was riding from Amelia Beach into Fernandina, on his bicyle, when near the residence of Jimmie Drummond he ran over an immense rattlesnake, which was crossing the road.

When the wheel came in contact with the snake it was thrown to the ground, and the snake immediately put himself in coil and struck at the boy, missing him with his fangs and striking the body of the bicycle, on which now can be seen their imprint. The body of the snake came in contact with the shoulder of the boy, who was almost paralyzed with fear. At about that time Drummond appeared on the scene and captured the snake, which was a tremendous one, being 8 feet long and fully 12 inches in circumference.

Newspaper piece on a chance encounter with Jimmy Drummond. *From the* Selma Times, *September 3, 1901, via Newspapers.com.*

Rattling Ghost Chains

Legend has it that a big tree stood behind Jimmy Drummond's home. An iron chain hanging from the tree had been there so long that the tree had partially grown around it. Buried treasure lay in the ground beneath. Sometimes, at night, ghostly hands could be heard shaking the chain. It's a localized version of an old legend about buried treasure, a legend explored in chapter 2.

Lay of the Land

This book doesn't tell Amelia Island's story in a linear fashion. Instead, it clusters stories by subject matter of interest. So, moving ahead, we should clarify something for readers who haven't yet encountered Amelia.

The relationship between Amelia Island and Fernandina Beach can confuse people, especially because the latter is often used in place of the former as though they are synonymous. The reason for that is because they are, in a sense, synonymous. Fernandina Beach is a city that covers the majority of Amelia Island. Southern Amelia contains the unincorporated communities of Amelia City and Franklintown, but when most people refer to Amelia Island, they're referring to Fernandina Beach.

When speaking on matters of commerce and culture, Fernandina Beach essentially is Amelia Island, though this book strives for clarity when a distinction between the two is needed.

Chapter 2

Castaways, Shipwrecks and Buried Treasure

The Gold Beneath the Sand

Buried treasure has indeed been found on and around Amelia Island. Qualified experts believe there's more out there—possibly much more, and possibly even one of the biggest loads of treasure to have ever been lost at sea.

Amelia Island was a stomping ground for notable pirates. Blackbeard, Captain Kidd and Jean Lafitte all passed through the area. Then there was the terrible Agramont, lesser known but notable for his savagery and the fact that his primary area of operations was around Amelia.

WARNING

In fullest disclosure, and out of severest concern for public safety, let it be known that a ubiquitous piece of wisdom holds that the attainment of pirated riches always comes at a terrible price. As the December 20, 1928 edition of the *Richwood Gazette* warned in a piece titled "Find Old Spanish Gold in Florida," "Tradition says pirate gold is bloody gold and he who finds it shall not enjoy it."

Those who find buried treasure are cursed for the rest of their days. (Un)fortunately, those days often wind up being very few. So if you've got gold fever, by all means indulge it. Just remember, friends, the old maxim to be careful what you wish for (and don't blame this author if ol' Bloody Bones comes a-knockin').

Oh, and bring a Bible…

Vintage postcard of a woman on Fernandina Beach looking at buried treasure. *Amelia Island Museum of History.*

Phantom Trees and Ghost Chains

Make haste if you see a large live oak with a chain hanging from it in Fernandina Beach. Legend claims that it marks a sizable treasure. People have claimed to have seen the tree but, on returning to the spot with shovels, found it vanished.

The tree and the chain aren't exclusive to the Amelia Island tale. Both appear in Robert Louis Stevenson's *Treasure Island* and other pirate tales. The story goes that buccaneers would mark their buried treasures with chains in trees. They'd kill a crewmate and doom his spirit to protect the treasure. It's further said that you must read from the Pentateuch (the first five books of the Bible) to banish the ghosts left behind to guard the glittery stuff.

The Fernandina legend has taken on a life of its own. It's usually tied to no particular pirate, but Fernandina-born author, World War I veteran, adventurer and journalist T. Howard Kelly connected it to the famed Captain Kidd.

Treasure Bearers Killed at Cache

Kidd stationed one man in the tree top with a lantern. He signaled the other members of the crew to come to the spot, one at a time and a half-hour apart, with a load of booty.

As each sailor buried his chest, he was murdered by the savage buccaneer and his devil-hearted aides.

Kidd is said to have marked the trees with a great anchor chain before he sailed away, only to be shortly captured and taken to England, tried, convicted and hanged, as history relates.

Ever so often the discovery of an anchor chain fastened to an Amelia Island jungle oak is reported. But I am convinced that Kidd did not leave such an obvious marked for his buried treasure. If I am not badly mis-

Newspaper piece discussing Captain Kidd's treasure. Pittsburgh Sun-Telegraph, *December 22, 1935, via Newspapers.com.*

Shortly before his arrest and eventual execution in 1701, Kidd anchored in the harbor off Fernandina about one hundred yards north of the site where Fort Clinch stands today. He led a clandestine landing party ashore to bury his booty. He then had his men carry armloads of treasure to a lantern-marked spot in the woods, one at a time, keeping a half-hour separation between them. Kidd executed each one after he arrived and tossed his portion of booty into the hole.

There's little evidence to support the story, but it's not inconceivable. Kelly didn't believe that Kidd would tie chains to trees he buried treasure under, because that would make it easier to discover, but he did believe Kidd left treasure behind.

The Expedition of T. Howard Kelly

T. Howard Kelly would deserve a section in this book even if he'd never hunted buried treasure. He's one of Amelia's most fascinating and accomplished sons.

Born on Amelia Island in 1895, son of a military family, he served as a noncommissioned officer in the 103rd Field Artillery, 26th Division. He saw action and was wounded in France. After the war, he became a writer of some reputation, penning news articles, war novels (his most prominent work being *What Outfit, Buddy?*), over five hundred short stories and film scripts for *Lover's Island* (1925) and *His Buddy's Wife* (1925).

According to a *Palm Beach Post* article from December 1934 titled "'Man is a Natural Warrior,' Says T. Howard Kelly, Writer of Well Known Works on the Recent Conflict," Kelly didn't live on Amelia full time as an adult. He spent months there while living in "a tiny lean-to, which he built himself, and there he goes to spend several months of each year to write and fish and bask in the sun, while a red pennant from his flagpole warns the world that he is at work and cannot be disturbed."

"ABOUT THERE"—T. Howard Kelly, another of the "gentlemen pirates," points out to Mrs. A. G. Peine, Chicago, a guest of the expedition, where pirate gold has been found.

Newspaper piece on T. Howard Kelly searching for treasure on Amelia Island. Omaha Sunday Bee-News, *December 22, 1935, via Newspapers.com.*

Kelly was fairly obsessed with tropical islands and buried treasure. In 1934, he funneled both of these passions into an expedition to find the aforementioned gold left behind by Captain Kidd. He was secretive about the location, but he described it as a place around one hundred yards from shore. "Our search will be in the jungle opposite this sea sector," he said.

The crew dug through various sections of the island and found some coins, mostly minor, but there's no indication that they found the big haul Kelly dreamed about. The expedition disbanded quietly, by all accounts. It's possible they found something more significant and kept quiet about it, but nearly one hundred years later, it seems unlikely such a secret could have been kept for so long.

Amelia Island Treasures Found Through the Years

Documented stories of people finding treasure on Amelia abound.

Schreck's Plenty: In 1928, four-year-old Wilhelmina Schreck found a can full of coins while making mud pies in her backyard. They were Spanish copper and silver tender from 1683 to 1772. Using a garden hose, her father, apparently an early twentieth century MacGyver, rigged up a sluice gate such as miners use. The Schrecks soon found themselves in possession of 1,700 coins, as well as human remains, arrowheads, and cannon ammunition. The value of the coins has been estimated at $1,800, which would be about $32,000 in today's money.

A 1935 news piece on the topic shared that the Shreck family left the area "immediately." We don't know what came of them—hopefully not the curse!

Gass and Pinkney: The December 22, 1935 edition of the *Pittsburgh Sun Telegraph* featured a story titled "Buried Pirate Gold Lures Expedition to Amelia Island Jungles off Florida." The story was based on an expedition led by John Charles Thomas and Amelia Island Treasure Expeditions. It reported that around 1900, two men named Gass and Pinkney found a chest full of seventeenth- and eighteenth-century coins worth around $20,000, which would be over $700,000 today.

AN UNNAMED FIND: Few people have done more Amelia treasure hunting than maritime archaeologist Scott R. Jensen. He discusses his findings in the *Amelia Island Book of Secrets*. One story he shares is about a treasure hunter who found a chest that Jensen believes to be from the 1700s. The box held a silver crucifix, gold nuggets and doubloons, silver coins, emeralds and silver. Outside of sharing his story with Jensen, the treasure hunter has chosen to remain anonymous.

THEY CALLED HIM MR. CRIBB: In 1924, Robert Cribb, who worked a shrimp boat named *Republic*, found a considerable amount of treasure after heavy rains caused part of a bank near Old Town to collapse. He dug the coins out of the resulting cavern. The money was in good condition, suggesting it had been carefully hidden for safekeeping rather than lost or tossed haphazardly. Each coin was over one hundred years old. Cribb gave one to his boss and vanished, never to be seen again. Some, predictably, blamed this on the pirates' gold curse, but there seems to be a simpler reason for a man who'd very publicly fallen into a considerable sum of money to disappear. Or, perhaps, someone got to him before he could get out of Dodge.

Aury's Gold

Later we'll discuss Louis-Michel Aury, a privateer who sailed to Fernandina in 1817 to help Gregor MacGregor "liberate" the island. For this section, we're only concerned with the man's gold.

Aury arrived at Amelia after Scotsman Gregor MacGregor's takeover had fallen apart. Aury was, ostensibly, a freedom fighter, but he wasn't averse to rewarding himself with some of the gains he came across in his adventures. He was a privateer, which was basically a legalized pirate commissioned by various governments to raid their enemies' ships. As such, Aury regularly captured loot taken from enemy vessels.

An exciting thing about Aury's gold is that we have good documentation that it really is on Amelia. Our evidence lies in U.S. Supreme Court records from the case of *Ex Parte, Madrazzo*, 32 U.S. 627 (1833). Those records state that a fellow named William Bowen purchased ninety-five slaves from Aury in Fernandina, after the United States had outlawed slavery. When Bowen tried smuggling them into western Florida, U.S. forces busted him. The slaves were claimed by the state of Georgia.

Bowen took to the courts to plead his case. It seems inconceivable to modern ears that a man would publicly argue for his "legal right" to possess other human beings, but such was the world in 1817. The primary loophole in the case was that the slaves were purchased in Spanish Florida, not the United Stated, so U.S. antislavery laws didn't apply. The courts decided that, regardless of any jurisdictional conflicts, Aury had pirated the "goods," and neither Bowen nor anyone else had any legal rights to stolen goods.

Through the court proceedings, we learn that Aury received $60,000 for the slaves, about $1.3 million today. It's known that Aury was broke when he left Amelia, leading to the reasonable conclusion that he buried at least some of his treasure before heading off. He ruffled many feathers in Spain and the United States and had good reason to believe that he might be attacked at sea.

The San Miguel*: A Ship Beneath the Waves*

All other stories of Amelia Island treasure pale in comparison to the story of the *San Miguel*. The treasure aboard the ship is well documented and estimated to be worth greater than $2 billion in 2023 money. That's no typo—it's "-illion" with a *b*, not an *m*.

HOW IT STARTED

The *San Miguel* was one of eleven ships in what historians refer to as the 1715 Treasure Fleet, which combined Spain's five-ship Flota de Nueva España and six-ship Flota de Tierra Firme fleets. It contained a twelfth ship, the French frigate *Le Grifon*, but that hit out for deeper waters and escaped the storm that sets the stage for this story.

History buffs' ears will perk up at the year 1715 because of the War of the Spanish Succession, which raged from 1701 to 1715 and saw Spain, Austria, France, Great Britain, Savoy and the Dutch Republic locking horns to see who'd win dominion over a Spanish empire that had been left without a ruler following the 1700 death of childless Charles II. The war had sapped Spain's resources. It desperately needed money from its colonies and outposts.

To that end, the fleet set off from Havana, Cuba, on July 24, 1715, loaded with treasure. At two o'clock in the morning on July 31, it got caught in a hurricane near Vero Beach in southern Florida. All ships were lost except for the previously mentioned *Le Grifon*. Over one thousand men lost their lives.

So if this is the case, why are we talking about treasure off the coast of Amelia? Well, there's good reason to believe the *San Miguel* escaped the hurricane.

How It's Going

The *San Miguel* was the fastest ship in the fleet, suggesting it would have been top choice to carry the Queen's Dowry, which consisted of massive stores of jewels, silver plate, gold goblets and coins and luxuries such as tobacco and spice. The treasure would have been substantial because it was intended to fund a war. In addition to being the fastest ship in the fleet, the *San Miguel* was seen shortly after the hurricane with its mast blown off, drifting north past St. Augustine. If sightings were accurate and the ship sank shortly after, it would indeed have gone down near Amelia.

Professionals still search for the *San Miguel* in the Caribbean, so not everyone is on board with the Amelia terminus thesis. But there's further reason to believe that it did indeed go down near Amelia.

In 1975, close to the south end of Amelia, amateur treasure hunters found twenty-two gold coins. Another discovery nearby clocked in eleven coins, these dating from the 1530s to 1540s. In 1989, an anonymous man turned up fifteen silver coins from 1715 at Little Talbot Island, just south of Amelia. In that same year, a man from Atlanta found twenty-eight coins. Cannons and a jeweler's furnace have also been scooped up in a shrimp net. These aren't slam dunks, but they give legitimacy to the possibility that the *San Miguel* sleeps beneath the waters off Amelia.

Qualified historians and treasure hunters such as Doug Pope and Amelia Research & Recovery are confident that the *San Miguel* is somewhere between St. Augustine and Amelia. They're so confident that they're willing to invest significant money, time and hardware into looking for it. Environmental regulations and red tape are the only things slowing them down. Modern treasure-hunting techniques use specialized vessels to blow holes in the ocean floor, kicking up anything that's buried beneath the sands, which is disruptive to ecosystems.

Perhaps a hurricane will someday turn up more remnants of the *San Miguel*'s treasure, or perhaps some treasure-hunting team will have a successful search. Until then, this is one piece of Amelia Island history that will have to remain hidden.

A Philadelphia Quaker in King Charles II's Spanish Mission

> *About One a Clock in the Moring* [sic] *we felt our Vessel strike some few strokes, and then she floated again for five or six Minutes, before she ran flat aground, where she beat violently at first; the Wind was violent; and it was very dark, that our Marriners could not see Land: The Seas broke over us, that we were in the quarter of an hour Floating in the Cabin.*
> —Jonathan Dickinson's Journal or God's Protecting Province

In 1696, an Anglo-Jamaican Quaker named Jonathan Dickinson shipwrecked on southern Florida shores with his wife, his six-month-old child and twenty-six others. They'd been traveling from the Bahamas to Philadelphia. A grueling march north took them to Amelia Island. Dickinson recorded his experience in a journal published in 1699 as *Jonathan Dickinson's Journal or God's Protecting Province*. The book gives us one of the best first-person accounts of Florida in that era and certainly one of the best of Amelia Island.

Dickinson was born in 1663, making him thirty-two or thirty-three at the time of his Amelia adventure. He and his fellow castaways were on a ship named *Reformation* when a storm blasted them ashore, hundreds of miles from the nearest European settlement. On their hike northward, they encountered the Jobé, Ais and Santaluces tribes, as well as some Timucua in settlements south of St. Augustine. Florida is known for its heat, but it was actually cold that most plagued the party. At least five of them died of exposure.

Despite Dickinson being a citizen of a British colony, the Spaniards in St. Augustine received him and his band warmly. They fed, housed and transported them to the Santa Catalina mission on Amelia, from which they could obtain further transport to the northern English colonies.

Father Francesco, head of the Amelia mission, reacted with uncertainty at the appearance of Dickinson's party. Unexpected visitors were a strange event in that corner of the world. Once assured they were no threat, he took them into the mission.

It was a dark time for Indians living in Santa Catalina. The person in charge, Ensign Diego de Jean, wasn't much of a man, much less a leader. He openly kept a mistress, which was particularly distasteful given that early Spanish missionaries had forced New World Natives to adopt monogamy, even to the point that it inspired a violent uprising among Guale Indians in 1597.

Adding insult to injury, Diego forced the Natives to keep his mistress's belly full despite the fact that food was scarce and hard-won. When the Natives refused, Diego barged into their homes and took the food right from their own stores. The mission was in low spirits at Dickinson's arrival.

Dickinson stayed in a guesthouse capable of fitting over three hundred people. With one long, central room and several segmented compartments with reed-mat beds, it was there both to house guests and to host group celebrations and events.

Dickinson described the Native women as having long, black hair and wearing moss sheaths similar to Greek togas. They used shell scrapers to shave corn from cobs, storing some and pounding the rest into meal. One reads this account and thinks of the archaeological expedition of the 1980s that turned up bones showing residents suffered from diets with too much corn and too little protein.

Despite the food shortage, the women rolled corn into fritters for their guests to eat on their way home. Within three days, Dickinson's party was ready to depart. Residents canoed them to British Carolina.

Dickinson's writing became less thorough as he moved north, so his account of Amelia is less richly detailed than some of his other stories. Still, we're fortunate that he recorded his travails. It's amazing to think of a man dragging himself through swamps and tangled forests and still having energy at the end of the day to write about it.

Chapter 3

An Island by Any Other Name

Lovelorn Princess Amelia

The life of Princess Amelia Sophia Eleanora reads like a Shakespearean tragedy. Her tale of star-crossed love is sad, but its poetry fits her namesake island's spirit perfectly.

Princess Amelia was born on June 10, 1711, in Hanover, Germany, the third daughter of Queen Caroline and King George II of Great Britain. He took the throne in 1727, when Amelia was about sixteen. He's primarily known for his crudeness, quick temper and rampant womanizing. His indifference to public opinion and expectations rubbed off on his daughter.

Princess Amelia would fit well into modern times. She'd likely be called a "badass." Her house was known to be ugly, dirty and full of dogs. She played cards (a scandalous hobby for women in her era), took snuff and hung out with stable hands. Yet she also gave a significant sum of money toward the care of orphaned children. She was assertive and politically active in her life, though unconcerned with the conventions of diplomacy and polite society.

Princess Amelia wasn't above some occasional blind selfishness. Immediately after being put in charge of Richmond Park in London, she shut it down to all visitors. Only a legal battle got it open again. She was her father's favorite, so much so that his final words, stated as he lay on the floor breathing his last, were, "Call Amelia."

Amelia's life should have been easy. She was born into royalty and the vast privileges that royalty brings. Yet material comforts didn't satisfy her. What

Princess Amelia of Great Britain (1711–86). *Wikimedia Commons.*

she wanted was the love of her life, Prince Frederick, son of Frederic William, the "Soldier King" of Prussia. Prince Frederick was a man of culture and the arts. His temperament clashed with that of his militaristic father. He matured into Frederick the Great, one of Europe's notable rulers, but at this time, he was a disappointment to his father. He stood up to his dad often and swore that he'd marry Amelia or no one else. The battle got so serious that Frederick's father cast him into solitary confinement and promised that he'd take away his son's inheritance if he continued to resist. Frederick had no choice but to obey. He married Elisabeth Christin and had no children.

The equally lovesick Amelia never married and never had children. She rebelled against the polite and formal world in which she was raised, forever seeing it as the hand holding the dagger that pierced her heart.

Amelia died on October 31, 1786. She's buried at Westminster Abbey.

THE MAN WHO NAMED IT

Princess Amelia provided the name and James Oglethorpe, first governor of colonial Georgia, the naming. He was scouting northern Florida in 1736 when he stumbled upon the island. We tell Oglethorpe's story in chapter 7.

AND IT SHALL BE CALLED FERNANDINA

Few would object to the poetic value of the name Fernandina, so it's something of a dirty secret that it stems from Ferdinand VII, whom history remembers almost universally as a base man with little concern for anything beyond maintaining his own power. Fernandina is a feminization of Ferdinand.

The name came from Governor Enrique White at a time when the town was known as Old Island Post. He officially declared the name on December 24, 1810, with orders that it be adopted on January 1, 1811. That wasn't White's only contribution to Amelia. He also made the wise decision of hiring George Clarke, a decision that would shape (literally) the city forever.

In 1951, Fernandina and nearby Fernandina Beach joined, keeping the latter's name.

NAPOYCA

The oldest known name for Amelia Island is Napoyca, given by Timucua Indians who lived there before Europeans came. We go into their story in chapter 4.

Chapter 4

Napoyca: Before European Eyes

Before Europeans laid eyes on Amelia, the Timucua Indians called it part of their home (southeastern tribes were mobile, so no one location singularly qualified as home). They called the place Napoyca. Thirty-five chiefdoms made up the Timucua. They occupied more than 19,000 square miles of land that now makes up northern Florida and Georgia. Their population on European contact has been estimated at two hundred thousand. They are often discussed as part of the "St. Johns culture," which is the name given to the various Native peoples living around the St. Johns River.

The Timucua didn't call themselves Timucua. The name was likely taken from the one that the Saturiwa chiefdom used for the Utina chiefdom. The Spanish adopted that name for all the Native tribes in the area, and the designation is still used today. The Timucuan people had extensive trade networks between their chiefdoms and connecting to other tribes.

The Timucua ate shellfish, turtles and much catfish, as well as birds, lizards and various mammals. They gathered berries, cabbage palm and nuts, while planting corn, squash and beans. They also cultivated tobacco and made bread from the koonti root. For religious ceremonies they drank "black drink," a caffeinated brew from yaupon holly trees.

The Timucua tattooed themselves to mark status and notable deeds. Those of higher social status were covered in tattoos by the time they reached adulthood. They did it by dotting holes in the skin and rubbing ashes into the wounds. Their clothes were made of moss and animal skins.

The Timucua were initially reluctant to deal with Frenchman Jean Ribault, the first European they had contact with, but eventually warmed to him. They became friends, in fact, despite Ribault's men severely taxing the Timucua's food reserves. Initially, Timucua were happy to trade food for things like metal tools, but eventually they couldn't keep up with the Frenchmen's needs. Still, despite those difficulties, they remained friendly enough that they showed animosity toward Pedro Menéndez after his Spanish soldiers slaughtered the French.

Despite their hard feelings over their former French friends, the Timucua were still approachable, but Spain quickly ruined that opportunity. To his credit, Spanish leader Pedro Menéndez seems to have made an earnest effort to establish good relations, but his men simply lacked the skill set for such diplomacy. When negotiations got tough, they reverted to their well-established game plan: to attack and intimidate. Relations went from strained to outright violent when Frenchman Dominique de Gourgues appeared, seeking vengeance against the Spanish. The Timucua happily aided de Gourgues in assaulting Fort San Mateo and killing every Spaniard present.

In time, things would change. Timucua (and other local tribes) would live in Spanish missions and develop close affinities with the priests and clerics who

Timucuan Indians at Ribault Monument. *Wikimedia Commons.*

lived with them. They would show loyalty to Spanish priests, in fact, despite it materially damaging their lives. Archaeological examinations of bones indicate the mission Indians lived hard lives and suffered from malnutrition, with too much corn and not enough protein in their diets. Why they would choose to live with the Spaniards given these facts is a mystery. Another mystery is the fact that, despite the malnutrition indicated by the bones, the mission Indians appeared to live longer lives than the pre-mission Indians.

The Timucua were extinct by the early nineteenth century, done in by a combination of European-borne diseases, war and losses to slave raiders from both Carolina settlers and other tribes.

An Old, Old People

The Timucua are believed to have lived in the area of Amelia Island as far back as 2500 BC, well over four thousand years ago. They were purely nomadic then, moving where the food was plentiful and the weather acceptable. They ate so much shellfish that they left behind giant "middens" made of their tossed-away shells. Some of these middens can still be seen today, and boaters at low tide will see massive oyster beds along Old Town's riverbank. There's also a Shell Midden Lane in Fernandina.

While Timucua were the primary residents of Amelia, records indicate that other peoples, known and unknown to history, passed through the area often. It was a hub of sorts, with various tribes staying over for brief times before moving on.

Timucuan Pottery

In Brazil, archaeologists have discovered ceramic pottery as much as 7,500 years old. The technique spread throughout South America. As far as the area that is currently the United States goes, however, the Natives of the southeast were the first to fire clay for pottery. Records indicate the practice going back as far as four thousand years ago.

Around 500 BC, an important discovery was made: the mud along the St. Johns River's shoreline was ideal for making pottery. With this new material, the Saint Johns People (as historians call the native ancestors of the Timucua)

The Florida Times-Union, Jacksonville, Monday, August 14, 1989

— Elizabeth L. Wilkinson/staff

Vicki Rolland and Lance Greene prepare to cover part of the Santa Catalina de Guale de Santa Maria site.

Amelia bones show tough Indian life

By James R. Ward
Staff writer

The 268 Guale and Yamasee Indians buried in 17th-century mission graveyards on Amelia Island were overworked and underfed, scientists have determined.

However, they still lived longer than their prehistoric ancestors, who were better fed and who didn't have to carry around burdens for the Spanish — a finding that is confusing researchers studying the remains.

Rebecca Saunders, supervising field archaeologist at the mission sites, said study of the bones at the sites indicated that the Indians' diets were nutritionally deficient.

The bones also reveal arthritis in vertebrae and feet, indicating that the Indians had been used to carry heavy burdens.

Researchers, however, are unable to explain why the Indians — whose remains were unearthed on Amelia Island four years ago — lived so long. Many lived to be 40.

The Indians who lived in the area about the year 1400 were better fed but rarely reached that age.

"It is a contradiction that we have not been able to solve yet," said Ms. Saunders, who is writing a dissertation on the Amelia Island missions for the University of Florida.

The Guale and Yamasee remains were unearthed at the sites of the mission graveyards of Santa Maria de Yamasee and Santa Catalina de Guale de Santa Maria, both within the Amelia Island Plantation.

The final season of the dig at the Santa Catalina mission began last week, Ms. Saunders said.

The excavations began four years ago, when a backhoe clearing land for a house uncovered the Santa Catalina graveyard.

Ten University of Florida archaeologists plan to spend their time between now and Oct. 27 completing the excavation of the convento, the house where the Franciscan missionaries lived; their kitchen in a nearby building; and a circular structure 70 yards north of the convento that might have been part of the mission village.

They also will try to locate the mission's church, which might have been situated over the remains of 150 Guale graves found earlier.

"The church may have been over the Guale graves because we have not been able to locate it elsewhere on the site. But we will dig a number of exploratory pits this season in an effort to find it," Ms. Saunders said.

The Guale came to Amelia Island in 1686, shortly after their mission village, Santa Catalina de Guale on St. Catherine's

(See INDIAN, Page B-3)

Newspaper article about an archaeological dig at the mission. *Amelia Island Museum of History.*

could make pots faster and of better quality than ever before. Because of this, people settled there in an unprecedented way, as far as archaeological records indicate. Sharing Napoyca were an estimated forty-six different Timucuan villages.

Chapter 5

Embargo This: Amelia Becomes a Dark Port

The Embargo Act of 1807 shaped the Amelia Island of its time.

President Thomas Jefferson and Congress signed the Embargo Act. Historians largely discuss it as a blunder, as it had deleterious effects throughout the nascent United States, including Amelia, but it's fair to note that Jefferson was dealing with a sticky issue. Despite coming out victorious from the Revolutionary War, the United States was still struggling to earn respect as a sovereign nation. Britain, particularly, continued trying to flex its authority.

Things came to a head during the June 22, 1807 Chesapeake-Leopard affair near Norfolk, Virginia. The British HMS *Leopard* attacked the American USS *Chesapeake* and took away four men for deserting the English navy. One man was hanged. The Royal Navy was short of sailors. To build reserves, England had enacted a law stating that citizens who signed onto the Royal Navy were lifetime subjects, meaning they were breaking the law by signing onto U.S. ships. The Chesapeake-Leopard incident wasn't the first or the only time that the British exercised this questionable interpretation of their law, but it was the tipping point. An outraged public demanded action.

Jefferson knew something had to be done, but he also wanted to avoid conflict. The nation was just coming together as a viable power, and a war could have been disastrous. He opted for economic warfare after diplomacy and official denouncement failed. He may have been naive in his thinking, as he thought the embargo would work because people would be willing to deprive themselves in the name of patriotism. This miscalculation was the primary reason the Embargo Act failed.

The act outlawed the exportation of American goods. The United States was already a strong agricultural center, and Jefferson thought he could hurt England at the dinner table. American cotton also went a long way in the English textile industry.

The problem was that without trade, Americans couldn't get luxury staples such as wine, sugar and coffee. England was hurt a bit by the embargo, but not nearly as much as Jefferson hoped.

The other problem was that there was an easy way around the embargo—and that way was Amelia.

Still owned by Spain, Amelia wasn't beholden to the Embargo Act. This fact quickly turned its idyllic port into a den of illicit trade, piracy and, eventually, slavery. People smuggled goods back and forth across the Georgia-Florida border. There wasn't an outright criminal mentality at first, just people trying to get things they wanted, but illegal activity attracts people who are comfortable working in the shadows. That's exactly what happened in Amelia. Soon, its harbor waters buzzed with baddies.

Things became dramatically darker when the United States made slave trade illegal in 1808. The goods coming into Amelia were no longer limited to pleasant luxuries. Now, the cargo included slaves. The United States' good intentions made things worse, in some ways. Patrols were given the authority to stop any ships suspected of carrying slaves, and the penalty for the captains of those ships was execution. The prospect of death made captains desperate to avoid capture, which led to horrors such as dumping whole shiploads of human "cargo" overboard.

Sometimes the slavers were smarter (and less brutal). U.S. patrols were only given the authority to search ships greater than five tons, so slavers switched to smaller ships. Or, anchored out of range, they'd have the slaves row themselves to shore, where they'd be picked up and taken overland into Georgia.

By the time the Embargo Act was ended on March 1, 1809, Amelia had already become a magnet for ne'er-do-wells. It would take time for the island to shake those ghosts, but she would do so.

(Some historians, namely Christopher Ward in his paper "The Commerce of East Florida during the Embargo, 1806–1812: The Role of Amelia Island,"* have called into question how extensive Amelia's illegal trade actually was.)

* *Florida Historical Quarterly* 68, no. 2 (October 1989), 160–79.

Chapter 6

Murderers, Marauders and Pirates

The Captain, the Pirate and the Governor's Son

On June 28, 1820, Captain John Jackson arrived in Fernandina searching for men of action. He needed reinforcements for his schooner, the *Dallas*, as he prepared to confront a man anchored outside St. Augustine in a ship believed to contain contraband African slaves—and Governor Coppinger's son, Cornelio.

The man, whose name wasn't yet known, had been promising to kill the boy unless his father sent food and water. Governor Coppinger, amazingly, refused the demands, leading to a dangerous faceoff that stretched on for days. Even without that dash of drama, Jackson would have been compelled to action. The United States had already declared slavery illegal.

Captain Jackson served in the United States Revenue Marine, established on August 4, 1790, to enforce federal customs law. The Revenue Marine's role expanded until it was renamed the Revenue Cutter Service on July 31, 1894. It was then rolled into the United States Life-Saving Service to form the Coast Guard in 1915.

This occurred shortly after the ouster of Louis Aury, when Amelia was technically held by Spain but put "in trust" by the United States. Jackson rounded up about a dozen men from Fernandina and led them out to sea. His ship, the *Dallas*, was a fifty-six-foot-long topsail schooner. Jackson had only been in command of the ship for a month, but he'd been a lieutenant aboard it in the past and knew it well.

Jackson had every reason to believe a confrontation was ahead, but when he got within sight, the nefarious ship pulled up anchor, lengthened sail and turned to flee. Its efforts were insufficient. Jackson's schooner was considerably faster and reached within a hundred yards of it by early afternoon.

Perhaps the ship's captain had been baiting Jackson in, or perhaps he simply changed his mind. Whatever the case, the strange ship turned to fight.

The two crafts bobbed up and down across from each other, each side manning cannons and muskets. In the end, the opposing crew decided that money wasn't worth their lives and refused to engage.

Jackson sent over a boarding party. They found 281 Africans in chains, clearly set for sale as slaves. An untold number of others were dead. As cargo, they'd be worth millions of dollars today.

The captain identified himself as John Smith. The ship was named the *General Ramirez*. Jackson brought Smith aboard. The questionable captain flaunted legal papers from Banda Oriental, the name formerly given to lands that currently make up Uruguay, Rio Grande do Sul of Brazil and parts of Santa Catarina. The papers suggested that Smith was a commissioned privateer, while the man claimed he'd merely anchored there because he was lost and needing supplies. Eventually, the truth emerged, mostly from his crew, who admitted the ship was actually named the *Antelope* and didn't belong to Smith at all. They'd captured it near West Africa.

Jackson arrested the crew on suspicion of piracy. His men took over the *Antelope*. Jackon and the Dallas led the commandeered craft to Savannah, Georgia, on July 24, 1820. He turned the Africans over to the U.S. marshal. Disturbing details emerged as it was discovered that the average age of the would-be slaves was only fourteen, and more than 40 percent of them were just five to ten years old.

What loomed ahead was an eight-year legal battle that went all the way to the Supreme Court and then congressional legislation, as the Africans had been legally purchased by a dealer in Havana, Cuba. The case was a significant one. It reached the desk of Chief Justice John Marshall, Founding Father and fourth chief justice of the United States, and shaped law for freed slaves for years to come.

Jackson's ship, the *Dallas*, was sold in Savannah in December 1821, at which point it dropped out of history.

Harmon Murray

March 16, 1891: By cover of darkness, the posse approached the outlaw's house on Tenth Street, Fernandina Beach. Deputy Sheriff Joe Robinson was among the men, most of whom were law officers or else otherwise accustomed to some amount of gunplay, yet their eyes nervously shifted back and forth. They may have been hunting that day, but the man they hunted was no passive prey. Just twenty-two, Harmon Murry had killed already and seemed hell-bent on doing so again. He was the boogeyman of Nassau County for some and the hero for others.

The posse circled the house. Murray had been cutting a swath of violence throughout northern Florida for months. He'd gone to Fernandina to hide at his sister's house and started robbing residents immediately. He was slick and fast, always one step ahead of Fernandina's lawmen, firing at them during at least one chase.

Robinson stepped forward, knowing it was dangerous but knowing, too, that he was sheriff. If anyone was going to take the lead, it would have to be him. He checked again to make sure the other men were in position and approached the house. As he crept around the porch, a gunshot blasted him off his feet.

With the fracas now begun, Murray made a break for it. Like a character out of an '80s action film, he leapt through a window, slinging bullets as he went, injuring Chief of Police James Higginbotham. With shots cracking in the air around his head, he disappeared into the wilderness.

The posse hit Murray with grazing shots in the scalp and wrist, but it wasn't enough to stop his flight. He escaped, as he had so many times already in his brief but action-packed criminal career. Sheriff Robinson died twenty minutes later. Fernandina put out a $750 reward for anyone who brought Murray back, dead or alive.

Having overstayed his welcome, Murray fled back to Alachua County in north-central Florida. His time in Fernandina was brief, but it ended with a bang.

Harmon Murray had his supporters. He was a desperado every bit as audacious as figures like Billy the Kid, but his name is rarely discussed alongside those of America's most infamous outlaws. For the people of northern Florida, though, in a time when news spread slower than rumors, his exploits were awesome enough to inspire people's imagination.

Murray wasn't a big man. About five foot seven, average for the era, the smooth-faced youngster was fast and athletic. He carried himself with a

'He had a Winchester rifle held at ready and a heavy pistol in his belt. Harmon Murray was looking for trouble.'

Image from a newspaper piece about Harmon Murray. Tampa Bay Times, *May 26, 1957.*

proud posture. Estimated to weigh around 145 pounds, he was quick to the draw and fleet of foot enough to elude a whole state.

Murray moved around northern Florida like a panther, disappearing for days or weeks at a time before reappearing in some new town or wildland. He escaped multiple close calls and broke out of a prison work camp. He popped up at a church supper once. When the servers nervously doled out smaller portions to him, hoping to expedite his departure, he shot twice into the ground, ate his fill and left an extra quarter behind.

Another time, a man bragged that he'd give fifty dollars for a chance to see Murray so he could shoot him. Murray got the drop on the fellow, said, "Now you see me, don't you?" and took fifty dollars from him. Once, a gun shop owner reached for a rifle as Murray entered. Murray drew, slapped his money on the counter and took the cartridges he'd come for.

Murray was also a Black man living relatively soon after slavery was ended, in an area experiencing deep racial tensions. When he was born, Blacks were the majority in his native Alachua County and wielded political power along with White, antislavery Republicans. The Confederate-sympathizing Democrat Whites had mostly left in disgust. Things had changed dramatically by the time Murray hit adulthood. The Confederate-sided Whites consolidated power and began organizing laws designed specifically to suppress African Americans.

Dynamics such as those made Murray a folk hero for some, and newspapers delighted in the sales-worthiness of a good old-fashioned folk hero. The only problem with that framing is that Murray didn't target only White people—not by a long shot.

Though many of Murray's crimes did specifically target Whites, he was not a purely racial killer. He abused plenty of members of his own race. In fact, his basic means of operation was to hold fellow Blacks at gunpoint and force them to go into town to get him food and supplies. Looking back, it seems that his fellow African Americans protected him more out of fear and an instinct for self-preservation than out of admiration.

Murray never lived to see twenty-three years old. On September 3, he went to Archer to "kill some crackers." He sought out an acquaintance named Elbert Hardy to help him secure firepower. The seventeen-year-old Hardy had attended a Gainesville rally at which he heard about reward money being offered for Murray's capture—and he set his mind to winning that payday.

Hardy accompanied Murray on his mission. At five o'clock in the morning, he shot him in the face.

The *Morning News* out of Savannah, Georgia, ran a piece on Murray's death titled "Harmon Murray Slain: The Terror of a Neighborhood Bites the Dust." It relayed the testimony of Alexander Hardy, the man who killed Murray. The article described the death in graphic detail. "He was shot with both barrels of a shotgun," it said, "loaded with No. 30 buckshot, each on the right side of the head, coming above the left eye, tearing the brain in pieces."

Authorities displayed Murray's body for public viewing, then embalmed and shipped it back to Fernandina, "so that persons interested…may view the remains."

The Killing of Deputy Jeremiah "Jerry" Mattox

Deputy Jeremiah Mattox was the first Black deputy in Nassau County. In 1950, he'd been given the position by Sheriff H.J. Youngblood, a man famous in some corners and infamous in others, in an attempt to ease race relations. Multiple events led to Youngblood's decision to specifically seek out an African American member of his force, but none more than a White deputy being violently attacked by a couple Black men, apparently for no other reason than being a White deputy. The environment had gotten so toxic and public sentiment toward police so bad that Youngblood knew he had to take action. Mattox was a respected World War II veteran and accustomed to operating under stressful circumstances, so he was a perfect candidate for the job, and Youngblood eagerly recruited him to balance out the racial demographics of his police force.

On March 13, 1954, Mattox drove to Eighth Street to check on a domestic violence report. He had no idea that he was walking into his own death.

As Mattox stepped out of his car, the very man he'd been called to check on stepped out and shot him. In a horrific coincidence, at that precise moment, Mattox's wife, Janet, arrived on the scene with some friends. They'd spent the day at the beach and were heading back to Janet and Jerry's home, two blocks from the site of the shooting. Janet saw Mattox get gunned down. The wound proved fatal.

Mattox and Janet had a child. Janet remarried, moved to Ohio, divorced and returned to Fernandina in 1984. In a bizarre and tragic tale, she was murdered three years later, on May 15, 1987. She was fifty-six years old and staying at 722 South Tenth Street, Fernandina Beach—directly across from the very house she'd been returning to on the day that she witnessed her husband shot down in cold blood.

Enter Jim Coe, Cold Case Detective

Solving murder cases seems like it should be easy in small towns like Fernandina, but complications came with Janet Mattox's case. False statements and a lack of physical evidence gummed the investigation up, and her death went unsolved for almost thirty years.

The police had suspects, particularly a man named James Lee Hall Jr., who was witnessed fleeing the scene. But they'd been unable to successfully put together a case amid a litany of false statements and a lack of physical evidence. Most damaging to a quick resolution of the murder was the false confession of Robert Jerome Way, who identified Octavian Troy Brewton as the murderer and himself as a lookout. Police arrested Way and Brewton on May 27, 1987.

The next day, Way failed a polygraph, which led to him admitting he'd made the whole story up. Police charged him with providing false information, and he went to the Nassau County Jail for six months. In hindsight, it was a small price to pay for being instrumental in giving Hall time to escape to Denver, which is what Hall did.

It wasn't until 2015 that Captain Jim Coe, retired Fernandina Beach police captain, solved the cold case. He'd been plugging away at it since his 2011 retirement. The work wasn't easy. Coe pored over the old evidence, noting that Hall had contradicted himself multiple times in questioning. In one example, he claimed he'd never been to Janet's house. He later claimed he'd been there to hang blinds and eat lunch. That was only one of numerous misstatements.

Reading Coe's findings, it's amazing that Hall slipped through the cracks, even considering Way's false confession.

Coe came away confident that Hall was guilty, but he needed DNA evidence to confirm his suspicion. That would be complicated. Hall had passed away from natural causes in 2000, and his remains were buried in Denver, Colorado.

Coe wouldn't be deterred. His work had already been exhaustive and exhausting, but he was determined to see it through. In addition to trying to piece together evidence that was nearly thirty years old, he dealt with the substantial legal complications inherent in retrieving old evidence. Some of Hall's family members also refused to cooperate.

Coe presented his evidence to a judge, who granted permission to obtain DNA from Hall's body. Forensic scientists showed that Hall was the guilty party in the killing of Janet.

In 1936, Janet was one of the original students at the Peck School; she graduated in 1949 as "Most Popular." She and Mattox married in 1950 at the First Missionary Baptist Church. She rests in Bosque Bello.

THE ASSASSINATION OF DR. ELISHA GRAHAM JOHNSON

When people think of Fernandina, things like "beautiful beaches," "quaint downtown" and "fascinating books of hidden history by The History Press" come to mind. Rarely do people think of political intrigue. Yet in 1875, Fernandina may have been home to a political assassination.

In 1875, the Florida state senate found itself stuck in a 12–12 deadlock, with equal numbers of Democrats and Republicans on each side. Neither side was willing to budge, and the situation dragged on. It seemed as though it couldn't be resolved unless one of the representatives died—and then one did.

Dr. Elisha Graham Johnson was born in North Carolina in 1839 and moved to Florida after the Civil War, in which he served as a major in the Confederate Army's Sixty-Ninth North Carolina Infantry division. He bought a turpentine farm and built it into a successful business. He served the United States Department of the Treasury as a deputy collector and was

Gravestone of Elisha Graham Johnson. *Amelia Island Museum of History.*

elected Republican state senator in 1870. He was initially declared the loser in that election, but courts reversed the call due to his opponent's supporters intimidating Black voters and other irregularities.

George McClanahan, a descendent of Johnson, says that the Ku Klux Klan threatened Johnson before he died. Johnson had joined the Republican party, which made him a traitor to the racist southern Democrats that dominated the area.

On July 21, 1875, Johnson was either a few miles from Fernandina searching for a still or had just closed his store in Lake City for the day (accounts differ). Someone shot him down in cold blood. His death broke the 12–12 tie. Two months later, an unnamed suspect was arrested and charged, but no known records tell how he ended up.

Johnson was buried in Bosque Bello. In 1921, his wife, Jennie, died. She may have been buried in the same plot with her husband. It's not a known certainty that Johnson was assassinated, but the coincidences in the case have left many historians wondering.

Jacksonville Mutiny and the Firing Squad at Fort Clinch

Public executions were rare on Amelia Island, with Merrick Jackson being a notable exception (Jackson is discussed in the section "Met Death Calmly and Died Easy: Merrick Jackson's Execution"). One ghastly event, however, saw six men cut down by a firing squad in Fort Clinch, three weeks before the first Christmas to follow the Civil War.

The story's inciting incident occurred on the morning of October 25, 1865. The Third Regiment, United States Colored Troops (Third USCT) had recently played a pivotal role in taking Forts Wagner and Gregg, digging trenches up to the target's parapets while taking fire and suffering numerous casualties.

The regiment was also dealing with a difficult mix internally, as some Black soldiers took umbrage at the orders of White officers. They were all Union, all fighting together to end slavery, but the dynamics were complicated. Rumors floated around about sadistic, unlawful punishments of Black soldiers in other units. Lieutenant Colonel Augustus Benedict, for instance, had covered men in molasses and tied them to stakes to be nipped at by hungry insects. Benedict was court-martialed and booted from the army, but that would hardly quell the concerns of other soldiers who saw themselves as potential victims of such harsh treatment.

From our modern perspective, it seems like common sense that there would be friction between Black soldiers and White officers, but we benefit from lifetimes of movies and books on the subject. People living of the time were struck by optimistic myopia. Their eyes were so fixed on winning the Civil War and ending slavery that little time or energy was left over to think about how such a sweeping social transition might actually look.

Turns out, the situation was rather complicated. On October 29, those complications and quiet resentments began to manifest, building toward tragedy.

On that day, in Jacksonville, a soldier was hung by his thumbs for stealing molasses. To hang a man by the thumbs, officers would strip him to his waist and tie his thumbs to a beam or something similar, letting the man hang so that just his tiptoes reached the ground.

White or Black, thumb-hanging had been a relatively normal military punishment. However, in his 1868 book *Military Law and Precedents*, military law attorney William Winthrop states that thumb-hanging was being phased out at the time and that it wasn't applied evenly among soldiers of all colors. Whether or not that's true, Black soldiers had spent their lives being unfairly punished by White men who legally owned them—and feelings around things like that don't die easily, it turns out. Saying "We're all together now" can't always erase such grievous indignities.

The soldiers didn't take the thumb-hanging quietly. Dissenters were led by Jacob Plowden, who had just completed thirty days living off bread and water in the stockade for threatening an officer with a musket over yet another thumb-hanging. Plowden had recently been promoted to corporal and, despite a minor disciplinary incident, had proven himself a reliable and worthy soldier. But Plowden also had a great deal of anger. He didn't like seeing White officers deliver corporal punishment to Black soldiers. In those circumstances, it's easy to imagine the Black soldiers doubting the sincerity of the White officers assuring them that these were standard punishments.

So, with all this volcanic emotion and uncertainty deep in the mix on that October 29 day, Plowden's angry refusal to watch a Black soldier hanged by his thumbs sparked a fire among twenty-five to thirty-five other troops. Angry condemnations and complaints grew to an outright battle that started with fists and graduated to gunfire.

Initially, the soldiers merely complained that the man had been hanging long enough and should be let down. When the officers continued, things escalated. Plowden grabbed his musket. Others followed. Plowden lowered his weapon and returned to his tent when ordered to, but the events had already been set in motion and taken on a terrible momentum of their own.

Lieutenant Colonel Brower fired first, launching three revolver shots at the approaching mob. Private Joseph Green took two of the rounds and fell. The armed soldiers told the unarmed ones to grab their guns. Soon, bullets were flying in all directions. The mutinous group remained only a small portion of the unit, and the Black noncommissioned officers tried frantically to get things under control. There were tussles among the Black soldiers, too, as some tried to suppress their compatriots.

In an moment of freakish irony, one bullet hit Lieutenant Colonel Brower in the thumb.

There were numerous other injuries, though not as many as one might expect when two groups of trained soldiers start firing on each other in close confines. Unfortunately, the bloodshed wouldn't end with the quelling of the mutiny. The worst was yet to come.

Fourteen soldiers were court-martialed. Six, including Plowden, were sent to Fort Clinch on the northern end of Amelia to be executed by firing squad.

On their final day on Earth, December 1, 1865, the men were agitated—except Plowden, who was openly defiant. Priests and ministers counseled and gave them last rites. The men were led to a plateau where six coffins waited, conspicuously open.

Plowden smiled. The soldiers who fired the shots were all Black members of the Thirty-Fourth Regiment. Some clerical figures stayed beside the men to the very end, offering solace and consolation. Their bodies were carried a short way to waiting coffins and dropped inside. They were buried on the spot, with no markers.

Centuries of erosion have cut through the island since then, dropping the bodies into the sea. Legal scholar John F. Fannin has explored the legal workings of the court-martial at depth in his paper "The Jacksonville Mutiny of 1865."

What Does This All Mean?

Mansion House and the Murder of F.C. Suhrer

Sitting in the relaxing silence of the Mansion Hotel's reading room in 1884, C.A. Key heard a scuffling sound. He closed his book and listened. The sound came again. Setting the book down, he went to the window. Outside, on the hotel's front porch, two men were grappling.

In the whirling confusion of bodies, Key heard one ask, "What does this mean?" Key recognized the voice. It belonged to Ferdinand Charles Suhrer, retired Union major and current manager of the Mansion Hotel.

Portrait of Ferdinand Charles Suhrer. *Amelia Island Museum of History.*

In answer to the question, a pistol shot flashed. Suhrer staggered backward. A shadowy man followed with two cracks of a whip.

Key ran for the entryway. He opened the door to see Suhrer on the porch, grasping the cracking end of a whip, the other end of which was held by Thomas Jefferson Eppes, who'd moved recently after living at the Mansion for years. In Eppes's other hand was a pistol.

Another eyewitness later described Eppes, a train conductor, as "a small man with small features."

Suhrer asked again, "What does all this mean?"

"You insulted my wife one week ago today," Eppes responded.

"I may be a dead man, Jeff," Suhrer said, "but before God, I did not."

A man named Captain Smith appeared. He took one side of Suhrer, while Key took the other. They led the man inside. The manager had been shot through his right breast. He was soon proved correct in his prediction that he was a dead man after succumbing to the wounds eight or ten hours later.

Eppes had been honest in his reason for killing Suhrer. His wife told him that Suhrer "insulted" her, by which it seems she meant he made a pass at her. Her claim sent him into a fit of rage. During the ensuing trial, it also came out that she'd made the whole thing up to make her husband jealous.

In a case of "things were very different then," the jury acquitted Eppes after learning of his wife's lie.

We know little of the Mansion House other than that it opened in 1871 and was one of Florida's hottest hotels in its heyday. It had all the era's most sought-after luxuries—including hot water in every bathroom! It burned down in 1887.

Like So Many Rats: Amelia Island Shipwrecks

Hidden beneath the waters outside Amelia Island lies the wreckage of at least forty-four ships. It's reasonable to assume that there are more, lost wrecks of undocumented and forgotten crafts whose crews died in anonymity. But the ones we know of are more than enough to provide some interesting tales.

(Note to readers: The *San Miguel* is the most important of Amelia's shipwrecks. It's discussed in the "Gold" section.)

Anonymous and Torn in Two

One unidentified ship was found torn in half. It appears to have been converted from a sailing vessel to a steamship at some point. The wreckage suggests that the ship's boiler room blew. The resulting damage, which blasted the entire craft into two, has led researchers to surmise that the boiler room explosion sparked ammunition stores being carried for the Civil War. Once that ammo went, the whole ship blew apart.

The Olivette

The Olivette was a steamship built in Philadelphia in 1887. During the Spanish-American War, it was put into commission to replace the *Relief* as a supply ship that would carry food, water and medical supplies to hospital ships in the war zone. It soon became a hospital ship itself, containing 280 beds. It was to carry sick and wounded soldiers out of the battlefields and into care at U.S. ports.

On August 31, 1898, a Wednesday, the *Olivette* pulled into the Fernandina quarantine station, holding multiple patients struck with measles and fever. A heavy storm hit. This was a couple months before the notorious hurricane of 1898, but the storm was severe all the same. By Thursday morning, the ship had gone down.

There were eighty people aboard, including forty-five crewmembers and thirty-five hospital staff. All of them escaped without harm, "but in scanty attire" (according to a September 7, 1898 account in the *Berwick Register*). Some rowed to a nearby schooner, others to the quarantine station. The ship sank in about thirty feet of water. One dramatic account out of the *Pensacola News* compared the people aboard to rodents: "Roustabouts sleeping in the lower holds had a narrow escape, being driven from their bunks like so many rats."

News stories mostly focused on the mystery of the sinking. Being a time of war, it was reasonable to be a bit paranoid. Today, though, the storm is widely acknowledged as being the cause of the sinking.

Met Death Calmly and Died Easy: Merrick Jackson's Execution

> *FERNANDINA, FLA., August 4.—Merrick Jackon, the murderer of John Thomas, was hanged here at half-past 12. The gallows was on the north side of the jail in the jail yard. The hanging was private, but there was a crowd of negroes around the jail. The drop was five feet. He met death calmly and died easy. There was no excitement.*
> —*"Blood for Blood,"* St. Louis Post-Dispatch, *August 4, 1882*

On November 19, 1881, Merrick Jackson grabbed his killing stick and headed to Kings Ferry. His weapon was a wooden club with lead packed at one end—simple yet sufficient to bash a man's brains in, as Jackson would soon prove.

No one is sure why Jackson went hunting that night. Newspaper articles covered his story but said nothing of his mentality. We know it happened. We just don't know why.

Kings Ferry still exists as an unincorporated community around the St. Marys River about a thirty-mile drive from Fernandina Beach. Up to the 1920s, it was one of the livelier areas in northeastern Florida. Jackson headed there during a festival. One has to wonder at the mind of a man who travels to such a celebratory event intent on killing people in the most brutal fashion possible.

Meanwhile, at the festival, George Ferguson and John Thomas were having a good time. Perhaps they knew Jackson was hunting for them. Perhaps not. We can't be sure.

Jackson had been stomping around, openly asking for Ferguson. Whatever plans he had in mind, secrecy clearly was not part of the design. On stepping out of a house and seeing the men talking to a woman in the piazza, he attacked.

BOB PATE'S GOVERNOR.

THE MAN WHO DISGRACES MISSOURI.

to concur in the Senate amendment giving $78,000 to continue the National Health Board.

Death of an Ex-Congressman.

BROCTON, MASS., August 4.—Artemus Hale, the oldest ex-Member of Congress, died last night, aged 98.

For Congress.

COLUMBUS, GA., August 4.—The Democrats of the Fourth District renominated Hugh Buchanan for Congress.

Renominated.

CHARLESTON, W. VA., August 4.—The Democratic Congressional convention yesterday renominated John E. Kenna by acclamation.

XLVII. CONGRESS.

Senate.

OFF FOR EGYPT.

Embarkation of British Troops Viewed by the Queen.

Threatened Strike of the Irish Constabulary—The Egyptian War—The Conference—Foreign News.

CONSTANTINOPLE, August 4.—Two transports started for Alexandria last evening with artillery and stores.

EMBARKING TROOPS.

PORTSMOUTH, August 4.—The transport Catalonia left to-day for Egypt, having on board Gen. Sir Edward Hamley, Gen. Sir Evelyn Wood and the West Kent Regiment.

BLOOD FOR BLOOD.

Three Murderers Pay the Penalty of Their Crimes on the Gallows.

Execution in Virginia and Two Hangings in Florida—A Respite—The Crimes.

Special to the Post-Dispatch.

FERNANDINA, FLA., August 4.—Merrick Jackson, the murderer of John Thomas, was hanged here at half-past 12. The gallows was on the north side of the jail in the jail yard. The hanging was private, but there was a crowd of negroes about the jail. The drop was five feet. He met death calmly and died easy. There was no excitement.

THE CRIME.

Merrick Jackson (colored) to be hung in this place this morning, August 4, for the crime of muder, committed at King's Ferry, Massau county, Fla., on the 19th of November, 1881. Merrick Jackson went to a festival held near King's Ferry, arming himself with a club, made of green wood, about two and a half feet long and about two inches in diameter, filled with lead at the butt end. On arrival at the festival he there caused a row and the testimony of several witnesses brought forth the following facts: That George Ferguson and John Thomas, two negroes from the State of Georgia, were sitting on the piazza of the house where the festivities were being held, talking to a negro woman, when Merrick Jackson came from the inside of the house asking for George Ferguson. As soon as Jackson saw Ferguson and Thomas on the piazza, he knocked them both in the head with his club, the blow knocking them off the piazza to the ground. Jackson then jumped out and standing over the prostrate form of Thomas, he dealt him several blows with the club, crushing in his skull, from the results of which Thomas died, Ferguson in the meanwhile getting out of the way. Jackson, not satisfied with what he had done, went to his home and procuring a gun returned to the scene of his butchery and by every conceivable means tried to find Ferguson, but was not successful, and returned to his house. The negroes in the neighborhood hearing of the crime became very much incensed, and during the night assembled, surrounded Jackson's house and captured him, bringing him here and safely lodging him in jail. Jackson was indicted by the grand jury of Nassau county on the 19th of April, 1882, tried and found guilty of murder in the first degree April 20, sentenced by Judge Baker April 21, and was hanged for the crime. This is the first hanging in Nassau county in many years.

Article on the hanging of Merrick Jackson. St. Louis Post-Dispatch, *August 4, 1882.*

Jackson's swift and brutal assault knocked both men down. He followed Thomas to the ground, raining blows onto the unconscious man's head until he was dead. While he did his grim work, Ferguson regained his feet and fled. On realizing his target had escaped, Jackson went home to get his gun.

News of the killing spread fast. The Kings Ferry community was enraged. If Jackson thought he could rely on closed lips from his fellow Black Americans, he was very wrong. They formed a crowd and surrounded his house. Showing remarkable restraint for the era and situation, they brought him to authorities.

Jackson was found guilty of first-degree murder on April 19, 1882.

Police hanged him in the enclosed yard. If the report of the event is to be believed, he died without drama. The community jail where he was hanged is now the Amelia Island Museum of History.

Chapter 7

Hoist, Lower, Hoist—Repeat

The Story of Amelia's Eight Flags

Eight different powers have flown banners over Amelia Island. We can't properly say eight different "nations" or "empires" because two of the flags (the Green Cross of Florida and the Patriot flag) belonged to individuals rather than proper governments, and a third falls into a gray category (Louis Aury's flag of the revolutionary Mexican Republic). Whatever their nature, these banners have led to Amelia being called the Isle of Eight Flags.

Each flag tells a story that could easily fill the entirety of a book—and, in some cases, already have. We'll delve into each one in the chapter ahead. The Timucuan Indians had no flags that we know of, so they are left out of this section and given their own.

Jean Ribault, French Florida and the Isle of May, 1562–64

[Ribault] *could do more in one year than others could do in ten, because he was the most skilled sailor and corsair known, very practiced in the Indies sailing and the Florida coast. —Pedro Menéndez de Avilés*

In 1513, Spain's Juan Ponce de León became the first European to officially discover Florida (it's possible others preceded him but left no documentation), but it was the French who established the original European settlement on Amelia. Specifically, it was a corsair named Jean Ribault.

French corsairs were privateers. They were legally entitled to keep a percentage of whatever treasure they looted from France's enemies at sea. Corsairs were an important force in the 1500s, and Jean Ribault was one of the very best.

Ribault's story was one of bravery and grit but, ultimately, one of tragedy. Much blood has been shed over Amelia, but no event produced more of it than the doomed quest of Jean Ribault and his French Huguenots.

Ribault Before Florida

Ribault was born in 1520 in Normandy. He was a seaman and a Huguenot—two facts that would define the arc of his life. The Huguenots were a sect of French Protestants that played an outsized role in world history. From 1562 to 1598, they fought the Catholics in the French Wars of Religion.

Ribault joined the French navy and served under Admiral Gaspard de Coligny, leader of the Huguenots. Though relatively scant, records of young Ribault paint the picture of a competent seaman and all-around impressive figure.

Perhaps no account of Ribault holds more weight than that of Pedro Menéndez de Avilés, for he's the man who eventually ordered Ribault's execution. Even after taking the Frenchman's life, Menéndez held Ribault in high esteem. In his laudatory writing, there may be an element of an ambitious man exaggerating the stature of his victory (a "big fish" tale), but Menéndez's respect for Ribault seems earnest. In a letter to Spanish king Phillip II dated October 15, 1565, he wrote:

> *I passed Jean Ribault and all the rest under the knife, understanding that thus it befitted the service of God Our Lord and of Your Majesty. I hold it to be a piece of very great fortune that this man be dead, because the King of France could do more with him with fifty thousand ducats than others could do with five hundred thousand. He could do more in one year than others could do in ten, because he was the most skilled sailor and corsair known, very practiced in the Indies sailing and the Florida coast. He was so much a friend in England, and had so much reputation in that kingdom, that he was named Captain-General of all the English fleet against the Catholics of France these passed years, when there was war between England and France.*

The Isle of May

In 1562, Coligny selected Jean Ribault to lead the settlement of a colony in the New World that would one day be the United States. Spain had sworn off Florida after failing three colonization attempts in 1526, 1559 and 1561. They had settlements in Mexico and Peru but deemed Florida too difficult to maintain.

Coligny was more than happy to take his crack at taming the land. He won permission for the voyage from Catherine de' Medici, queen of France. She granted it despite being Catholic. Catherine knew that if things went well, she'd wind up with a profitable colony, and if things went badly, she'd get rid of some Huguenot opposition. Catherine also wanted to test Spain's reaction to the presence of France.

The late 1500s were a time of European powers competing for treasures and lands, but Ribault's first voyage to Florida appears to have mostly been about religious freedom. Coligny wanted a place for the Huguenots to safely practice their faith, as Catholic France was becoming increasingly hostile. It's generally accepted that this was the primary motivator in both of Ribault's voyages to Florida, but some historians disagree. M. Adele Francis Gorman, for example, wrote a piece titled "Jean Ribault's Colonies in Florida" in the *Florida Historical Quarterly*[*] suggesting less noble inspirations behind the scenes.

Whatever the case, Ribault struck out with 150 soldiers and artisans on February 16, 1562. On May 1, 1562, he made it to the mouth of St. Johns River, where he left a stone column claiming the territory for France. Dubbed the Ribault Monument, a reconstruction of the object stands at the Fort Caroline National Memorial site in Jacksonville.

From the St. Johns, Ribault traveled north, mapping locations and looking for places to settle. Along the way, he found Amelia, still called Napoyca by the Timucua Indians. He was struck by its beauty and named it the Isle of May.

The Timucua invited the Frenchmen ashore and showed off their homes. A good bit of what we know of the Timucua comes from Ribault's accounts. Through his writings, we get a feel for the island:

> [We] *enterd and veued the cuntry therabowte, which is the fairest, frutefullest and plesantest of all the worlde, habonding in honney, veneson, wildfoule,*

* Vol. 44 (July–October 1965).

forrestes, woodes of all sortes, palme trees, cipers, ceders, bayes, the hiest, greatest and fairest vynes in all the wourld with grapes accordingly, which naturally and withowt mans helpe and tryming growe to the top of okes and other trees that be of a wonderfull greatnes and height.

Despite his fondness for Amelia, Ribault established a settlement named Charlesfort (in honor of Charles IX, king of France) on Parris Island. Satisfied he'd set things in motion, he headed back to France, leaving twenty-seven men behind. He planned to get supplies and return posthaste, but history had other plans.

Ribault returned to France to find that the tensions between the Catholics and Huguenots had reached a boiling point. The French Wars of Religion had begun. By the time they ended six years later, upwards of four million people lay dead from violence and deprivation.

Ribault fought for his Huguenots and nearly met his ruin when the port city of Dieppe fell. He wasn't a low-profile gentleman who could fade into the countryside, so he fled to Britain and asked Queen Elizabeth I to fund another settlement effort in the New World.

Above: Ribault Monument. *Amelia Island Museum of History.*

Right: Drawing of Jean Ribault arriving in Florida. *Amelia Island Museum of History.*

Elizabeth thought highly of Ribault and used him for various purposes, but something went wrong. Details are thin. We know Ribault did something contrary to his promises to the queen and fled. Her forces caught him and tossed him in the Tower of London. His detention takes him out of our story for a while, but it also gave him time to write a long account of his journey, which became invaluable historical material.

In Ribault's absence, the group at Charlesfort disintegrated. Soldiers mutinied, killing Captain Albert de la Pierria. A fire took out most of their supplies. Desperate, they built a simple vessel and set out for France. Their trip proved horrific as they resorted to drawing lots and eating whoever lost. Some boatmen did survive all the way to Europe, where they were rescued by a passing English vessel.

Among Them Were Gentlemen: Rene Goulaine de Laudonnière and Bloody Fort Caroline

Jean Ribault was still in prison when the French Catholics and Protestants signed the Edict of Amboise, which kept peace in France for a few years. Coligny, able to resume his place at court, started working toward a new expedition. He could no longer justify it with religious freedom because the edict, ostensibly at least, ended the Wars of Religion.

With Ribault gone, Coligny selected Rene Goulaine de Laudonnière, who struck out and made it to Florida on June 22, 1564. Laudonnière met a friendly Timucua chiefdom known as the Saturiwa, who displayed a shrine they'd made around Ribault's aforementioned monument. Laudonnière's French traded tools like knives, axes and scissors for food, but eventually, the Timucua couldn't satisfy the demands of their visitors. They didn't have enough food to support everyone. The French had no real choice other than starvation, so tensions rose.

Laudonnière and his crew found a spot on the St. Johns River and began building Fort Caroline on June 22, 1564. Laudonnière sent some men home because they were complaining about how hard the work was. They'd signed up for adventure at sea, not hard labor.

Many of those who stayed weren't happy either and deserted the camp to become pirates. Seventy of them held Laudonnière captive on December 18, forcing him to sign documents authorizing their departure. Others took it upon themselves to make harsh demands of the Indians. The settlers who stayed with Laudonnière were reduced to diets of roots and acorns.

Eventually, Laudonnière accepted it as a lost cause and sought to escape. He bought food and a ship from a passing privateer named Sir John Hopkins. On August 15, he completed preparations to sail home. He was only waiting for a good wind. History often turns on such small details. Subsequent events would have ended very differently if only for better weather.

Alas, as Laudonnière was readying to leave, Ribault arrived. He carried papers declaring that he was to assume charge of the settlement and offered to keep Laudonnière in charge of Fort Caroline. Laudonnière fell severely ill while they unloaded supplies from Ribault's ship and was bedridden for a week. His experience at Fort Caroline hadn't been a good one, but he had no idea how bad it was about to get.

A Spanish fleet appeared. Ribault left Laudonnière to defend Fort Caroline with 150–240 men (estimates vary), a mere 20 of whom were soldiers, while Ribault attempted a naval offensive.

On September 20, the Spanish shocked Fort Caroline with an overland attack. Because of heavy rain, some guards abandoned their posts to take shelter. The Spanish had only to take out a single sentry. With that, they spilled into Fort Caroline and did the grim work they'd come to do.

"They made a pretty butchery of it," one of the survivors later wrote.

The Spaniards put the men to the sword but spared the women and children, who totaled about sixty. According to Menéndez, a pikeman wounded Laudonnière as he escaped with about forty-five others. They fled to the mouth of the river and boarded a ship captained by Jean's son, Jacques.

The Spanish invaders opened fire and sank one of the French ships when negotiations failed. Laudonnière wasn't going to wait to see how things played out. He took one of the smaller vessels and headed back to France, reaching his native soil in mid-November.

Laudonnière went on to work as a merchant mariner. He died in 1574. In 1586, his memoir *L'histoire notable de la Floride, contenant les trois voyages faits en icelles par des capitaines et pilotes français* (*The Notable History of Florida, Containing the Three Voyages Made There by French Captains and Pilots*) was published.

Massacre at Matanzas

After being released from the London Tower, Ribault made it to France and set off for Laudonnière's settlement. He made it there with five hundred soldiers and artisans and seventy women. Four of his ships were too big to enter the harbor, so he left them at the mouth of the river. These ships were the first to spot (and to be spotted by) the Spanish.

At midafternoon on September 4, lookouts spotted five sails approaching from the south. Limp winds prevented the ships' flags from unfurling, so the lookouts couldn't see Spanish markers.

On the night of September 4, the Spanish attacked the anchored French ships. Ribault escaped, partly because the Spanish vessels weren't fully repaired from damage they'd taken during a hurricane. Ribault had soldiers and ships placed to deter potential naval assaults while preparing his own offensive. His plan was to attack the settlement that the Spaniards had set up in St. Augustine. Laudonnière didn't like the plan but couldn't stop it.

Unknown to Ribault, Menéndez was leading an overland force to Fort Caroline as Ribault set off to lead a naval assault. Disastrously unaware of Menéndez's land offensive, Ribault led two hundred seamen and four hundred soldiers aboard ships. They made it to their target on the morning of September 10. The Spanish shelled up without taking any damage, but effectively fell under French containment. It was pure chance (though the Spanish probably considered it an act of God) that the tide flipped when a tropical storm blew in and scattered Ribault's forces.

The winds pushed the French ships toward the shore. Nearly all of them wrecked or became stranded in shallow waters. A smaller ship escaped the weather and headed for the Caribbean, while the flagship *Trinite* grounded but remained functional.

The castaways found themselves in hostile territory as Indians harassed and attacked them. They created two defensive groups and headed for Fort Caroline, oblivious to the fact that their one beacon of hope was still wet with the blood of their friends.

One of the groups gathered at an inlet. Having been tipped off by local Indians, Spanish forces got to them on September 29. The French offered to surrender after hearing about Fort Caroline's demise. Menéndez cryptically replied, "Surrender your arms and place yourselves at my mercy, that I may do as Our Lord may command me."

The French ferried over the river. Menéndez removed from the group a pilot, four skilled tradesmen and twelve seamen who said they were Catholic and had been forced into service. The rest he had led behind sand dunes and put to the knife.

Ribault's group numbered as many as 200 (150 is a commonly held number). They found their own way to the inlet where their companions had recently been slaughtered, having no idea what had happened there. Menéndez led 150 soldiers to the inlet on October 11, 1565.

In a scene worthy of cinema, Ribault carried a truce flag to discuss surrender with Menéndez. Menéndez, however, would allow no such terms and stated that there were but two possible outcomes—either his men tracked down and killed Ribault's forces, or Ribault's forces threw themselves on Spain's mercy.

Ribault led about half of his force into surrender. The other half fled southward to take their chances in the wilderness. Menéndez slaughtered Ribault and his men. With that, he cemented Spanish authority over Florida.

Today, the location is known as Matanzas Inlet. *Matanzas* is Spanish for "massacre."

French Vengeance

To call Dominique de Gourgues a man of action would be an understatement. The guy sold everything he owned in order to buy three ships and lead a quest of vengeance against Spain, a full three years after Ribault's murder. He already harbored vicious hatred for Spain because he'd once been imprisoned by Spaniards and forced to work like a slave on a galley ship. Diplomacy was not an option. Nor was a peaceful compromise. He outfitted eighty men with a crossbow and a pike each and went hunting Spaniards.

In April 1568, de Gourgues set off for Spanish Florida. He made contact with the Timucua, who were ready to fight almost immediately. The wealth of gifts he'd brought for them was unnecessary, as the Timucua despised the Spanish already because of the harsh treatment they'd experienced from the Spanish and because of their old bonds with the French, which were still fresh enough to be remembered. Pierre de Bre, a Frenchman who'd escaped Fort Caroline and joined the Timucua, appeared. He knew the Timucuan language and acted as an interpreter for de Gourgues.

De Gourgues attacked San Mateo, which was the name Spain gave to the captured French Fort Caroline. Pedro Menéndez was gone, having traveled back to Spain to meet with the Crown. With help from the Saturiwa and Tacatacuru Timucuan tribes, de Gourgues killed every Spaniard present. The surrendering Spanish were shown precisely as much mercy as Ribault's men had been shown—which is to say, none at all. De Gourgues and the French put each man to pike or else hung them from trees.

Picture of Dominique de Gourgues. *Amelia Island Museum of History.*

De Gourgues had been considering keeping San Mateo on capturing the fort, but that was rendered impossible when one of the Timucua blew the place to bits. The Indian was cooking fish on shore after the battle and accidentally lit a trail of gunpowder as though he was a character in a Road Runner episode. The ignited powder ran into the fort and destroyed the structure.

De Gourgues' Frenchmen combined with his Timucuan forces might have been able to take St. Augustine from Spain as well. That wasn't de Gourgues' plan, though. He wanted revenge, and he got it. He traveled north. Days later, Pedro Menéndez returned to the site.

We know little about de Gourgues outside of this feat. He was a soldier, nobleman and military captain. He was also Catholic, not Huguenot, which gives an interesting twist to the story.

France never again exerted any significant influence on the affairs of Amelia or Florida.

FORGED IN BLOOD: FIRST SPANISH AMELIA

With the lowering of the French banner in 1565 came the hoisting of the Cross of Burgundy with its white background and red saltire—a saltire being a cross that's "tipped over" like the letter *X* (the Florida state flag has a saltire). Starting in 1506 with Philip the Handsome, Duke of Burgundy and first Hapsburg king of Castile, various Spanish rulers used the banner.

The man that brought the flag to Amelia was Pedro Menéndez de Avilés, butcher of Jean Ribault and his Huguenots. Menéndez jumps out at us from both first- and third-person writings of his era as an uncommonly resolute person. All personal shortcomings aside (a remarkable aptitude for unthinkable violence being one such shortcoming), it takes a person of incredible fortitude to colonize an area that had turned away so many attempts already. Menéndez was such a man.

Yet the story of Spanish Amelia isn't only the story of Menéndez. The history of Amelia is, in fact, largely a Spanish one. Spain ruled the island from 1565 to 1763 and again from 1784 to 1821. In doing so, the Spanish gave Amelia a unique history set apart from the course of events that make up the bulk of early American history.

Santa Maria, Spanish Amelia

Centuries after the events, Colonial Spain remains notorious for its brutal conquistadors. Yet even as they replaced the French flag with the Cross of Burgundy and named the island Santa Maria (hereinafter called Amelia), Spain was slowly transforming into one of the most humane of the European powers, with a concerted mission to care for Indigenous peoples.

Pedro Menéndez even made an earnest attempt to befriend the Timucua living in Florida. It was an uphill battle because the Timucua had considered the French to be friends. Menéndez's men also were ill-suited to delicate negotiations, reverting to their natural state as marauders whenever they reached a diplomatic impasse. In the end, despite his best intentions, Menéndez proved no friend of the Natives.

Spain's self-reflection started in 1537 with the writings of a Dominican friar named Bartolomé de las Casas. Casas's works highlighted the brutality of the Spanish conquistadors, which he personally witnessed.

Because of Casas's influence and legal efforts, Spain started rethinking its expansionist philosophy. The Indigenous peoples of foreign countries

Drawing of Pedro Menéndez. *Amelia Island Museum of History.*

were declared to be every bit as human as Spanish Catholics and, therefore, deserving of humane treatment.

So Menéndez might have taken Florida by cannon shot and sword, but it was Spanish Catholic priests who rooted themselves there to minister to the Native peoples. Forcing one's religion on others offends modern temperaments, but the Spanish priests did at least prove themselves sincere in their desire to save souls. The clerics endured terrible heat, discomfort and deprivation to perform their duties. Despite having considerable influence and privilege back in Spain, they chose to live in harsh conditions, acting as defenders of the Native peoples and liaisons to with Spanish political authority.

Despite best intentions, the mere presence of Europeans was killing the Natives, who had no immunity to European diseases like smallpox. Neither the Natives nor the Spanish understood what was happening. Communicable diseases were a mystery at that time. The priests misread the cause of outbreaks even as they attempted to minister to the victims.

Though exerting considerable influence, the priests weren't the only Spanish forces in Florida. Spanish governors, with aims less ethically lofty, demanded that Amelia Natives grow food for the Spanish in Saint Augustine. In exchange for this service, the priests pushed to have Natives recognized as official Spanish peasantry, putting them at the bottom of the social order but still in a better position than slaves.

The Natives seemed to appreciate their relationship with the Spanish priests for reasons that are still something of a mystery. Archaeologist Clark Spencer Larsen (author of *Essentials of Biological Anthropology*) did some work on Amelia in the 1980s, producing a paper titled "Human Remains from Mission Santa Maria, Amelia Island, Florida: The 1985 Season." His evidence suggested that Indians worked tremendously hard while suffering from poor diets, likely because their mission work kept them subsisting on maize without traveling to find sources of protein.

Knowing this, people have wondered why the Natives chose to remain on at the mission. They might have stayed because so many of their people were dying of mysterious ailments, while the Spanish seemed immune. Or maybe something in the Spanish presentation of Catholicism may have connected with them. We'll never know for sure.

In 1602, the Spanish built a church on Amelia, which was populated almost entirely by Timucuan Indians led by a chief named Gaspar. Named Santa Maria de Sena, the church attracted 112 regular attendees. Sermonizing was Fray Baltasar López, who regularly canoed in from Cumberland Island. López was a devout man who wrote about his Timucuan flock with pride and enthusiasm.

The next few decades were interesting, uncertain times in Amelia. The 1670 Treaty of Madrid officially recognized property designations between Spain and England, but it left the area bordering Spanish Florida and English Carolina in ambiguity. England had established a colony in South Carolina in 1663, putting English and Spanish settlers right in each other's faces and practically guaranteeing conflict. Spain maintained mission settlements on various barrier islands around Amelia and the coastal mainland, but the enterprise was doomed.

England armed and funded the Westo tribe to harass Spain and its Native allies while pirates prowled the waterways, snaking between the barrier islands. Frenchman Michel de Grammont was particularly active in his raids of Spanish settlements. By 1675, Yamasee Indians and their Spanish allies were Amelia's only remaining residents, while the Natives from northern settlements were under constant duress. They'd moved from the old bluff-front settlement to a safer marsh-front site beside Harrison Creek on the south side of the island—away from the immediate dangers of the northern raiders.

Eventually, the Westoes and pirates forced the Spanish-allied Natives southward. Amelia was close enough to Spanish power that it escaped most of the raids, but it wasn't immune to their aftereffects. In 1680, the governor of Spain ordered the Yamasee to replace the Guale Indians who had fled Santa Catalina (near Savannah) after the English attacked it.

The Yamasee agreed to head north alright but went right past Santa Catalina and back to the lands from which they'd come. They weren't foolish. They understood that going back to Catalina meant death or enslavement. With that, Amelia was left without a settlement for several years.

In 1685, the direction of immigration reversed. Governor Márquez Cabrera (who was removed from his post on April 11, 1687, for mistreatment of those under his care) tried to salvage what he could of the Spanish mission system as pirates and England's proxy forces tore through it. He needed refuge for Gaule Indians stuck on a vulnerable mission named Santa Catalina de Gaule. Cabrera saw an opportunity to solve two problems at once by repopulating Amelia with the Gaule.

In 1686, Father Francesco Simon de Sales resettled the Gaule with their chief, Micoa, on an Amelia that was home to two settlements: San Felipe and Santa Clara de Tupiqui. Micoa's ancestors had already been forced out of their mobile way of life when the hunting grounds they once traveled freely became filled with hostile forces. With the move to Amelia, they abandoned their ancestral grounds for good.

Once on Amelia, Micoa and de Sales found the dilapidated, overgrown church that the Yamasee had abandoned beside Harrison Creek. Rough as it was, it appeared like an oasis in the desert to the homeless party, and the newcomers set to work reviving the structure. They named it Santa Catalina de Gaule, Spain's northernmost mission.

In 1688, the crown ordered that a watchtower be built to protect Amelia. Florida governor Laureano de Torres y Ayala chose to divert that money to a St. Augustine seawall in a decision that proved disastrous in 1702, the year that the Spanish mission system effectively ended through the attacks of Carolina governor James Moore.

Spain eventually repelled Moore, but not until the cultural landscape had been permanently transformed. English rule would come, but Spain held for the next sixty years, even managing to entice a sizable number of Creek Indians to settle the areas abandoned by Timucuas and Apalachees.

The Sun Sets on the First Spanish Amelia

England and France went to war in 1754. Spain got froggy and decided to use the conflict as an opportunity to take advantage of England. In 1761,

Spain allied with France. England seized the Spanish-held port of Havana, which was critical to Spain's overseas empire. To get this back, Spain had to give up Florida.

With the 1763 Treaty of Paris, Florida officially became an English holding. The estimated 3,046 Spaniards there represented a power that had been running the place for nearly two hundred years. Yet just like that, England took control of Amelia and kicked them to the curb.

In an amazing display of humanity, Spain moved not only all its Spanish residents to Cuba but also all the Florida Indians that were with them. The Spanish priests saw themselves as guardians of the Native people. Yet for all their good intentions, the millions of Florida Indians had been reduced to less than one hundred by European diseases like smallpox—it's a tragedy that boggles the imagination.

AN AMELIA ISLAND AFFAIR FOR THE AGES: THE BALLAD OF GREGOR MACGREGOR

A strange banner flew over Amelia Island in 1817—a simple green cross impressed over a white background. It wasn't strange in its design so much as strange in that it represented no known empire.

It was called the Green Cross of Florida. It represented not a nation so much as a man. His name was Gregor MacGregor and, for better or worse, he was one of most interesting people to ever step foot on Amelia Island.

MacGregor Before Amelia

Gregor MacGregor was born on December 24, 1786, into the Highland Scottish Clan MacGregor. From 1803 to 1810, he fought the Spanish in the Peninsular War as an officer in the British army. In 1812, he joined "El Libertador" Simón Bolívar and his republicans in the Venezuelan War of Independence, during which he distinguished himself and earned the rank of general.

Truly, few men have ever mingled the roles of legitimate military servicemember and conman with such fluidity. MacGregor's exploits created ripples touching North American, South American and European shores. He enters our story in 1817, when a peculiar series of events led

Drawing of Gregor MacGregor. *Amelia Island Museum of History.*

him to liberate an island that didn't want to be liberated and to establish an illegitimate state that would evaporate as quickly as it was made.

An Amelia Island Affair for the Ages

The Embargo Act of 1807 turned Amelia into a magnet for lawlessness and dubious characters. Things worsened after the United States declared slavery illegal, turning Spanish-run Amelia into a port for trading slaves that could be smuggled up into Georgia. Distracted as it was with global events, Spain didn't have the resources to get things under control. By 1817, Amelia was ripe for a strongman to swoop in and take things over.

Simón Bolívar and the Venezuelan armies shaped MacGregor, who was only twenty-five years old when he joined them. He helped Bolívar overthrow Spanish power but found himself unwelcome by the people because he wasn't a Native South American. So he sought other ways to spread the "glorious cause."

With the etchings of a plan in mind, he sailed to Philadelphia. There, he was able to contact Lino de Clemente, Pedro Gual and Martin Thompson, representatives of Mexico, Rio de la Plata and New Granada—places resisting Spanish control. On March 31, 1817, the trio commissioned MacGregor to carry "into execution an enterprise so interesting to the glorious cause in which we are engaged: to procure both the Floridas, East and West" (according to *MacGregor's Invasion of Florida*, by T. Frederick Davis). His conquest would start with Amelia.

MacGregor was technically an Englishman conducting foreign military business in United States territory, a decision that would eventually come back to bite him. For now, he reacted to this by cutting the problem off at the pass and heading to Baltimore, where he struck up an association with the postmaster, who wrote a long letter encouraging John Quincy Adams to back MacGregor.

It could be argued that MacGregor had ample justification for his plan, as harebrained as it seems in hindsight. He thought he'd have full U.S. support once the government understood the wholesomeness of his intentions. He also imagined he'd be given a hero's welcome on arrival, since the Spanish had allowed Amelia to become "a channel for the illicit introduction of slaves from Africa into the United States, an asylum for fugitive slaves from the neighboring States, and a port for smuggling of every kind" (according to James Monroe's "Message from the President of the United States" of December 2, 1817).

MacGregor sold land receipts to fund his venture. He promised to repay investors with Florida property on his victory. With the funds, he built a force of wandering street toughs from Savannah and War of 1812 veterans from Charleston, numbering up to 150 men—which quickly dwindled to 55, partially because the men disagreed with MacGregor's passionate desire to end African slavery. MacGregor didn't plan on using only the forces he'd mustered. He thought that discontented rovers along the Georgia-Florida border would join his "glorious cause" once he arrived.

MacGregor won early support from a Fernandina landowner who was willing to act as a spy. The man informed MacGregor that Fort San Carlos, which was then protecting Amelia, was manned by aged Spanish veterans, poorly outfitted and led by the soft Francisco Morales, who seemed more a man of leisure than a military one.

On June 29, 1817, MacGregor led his little navy to the waters off Amelia's north end. He instructed a fisherman to notify Fernandina that their conqueror had arrived. He led fifty-five musketeers ashore to the area that is now Fort Clinch State Park, where they met the worst opposition they would face in the form of buzzing, biting insects that they tried fending off with sprigs of dog fennel.

They next traversed the sucking muds surrounding Egan's Creek and then the creek waters. Despite what must have been a chaotic scene, the men maintained discipline to break up into small groups in order to make the size of their force appear much larger than it actually was.

The ploy worked. Morales surrendered, thinking he was looking upon the advance forces of a much larger army. Not a man was harmed on either side. MacGregor hoisted the Green Cross of Florida and banished Morales to St. Augustine.

MacGregor took naturally and enthusiastically to the role of Amelia's celebrity liberator. He ordered a printing press and made Florida's first currency and newspaper. He took over Morales's former house and began issuing orders. With pomp and ceremony, he had special armbands made for his men, proclaiming, "Love live the conquerors of Amelia!"

Few others bought into MacGregor's grandiosity. He had some lukewarm supporters, but most of the residents simply left for the mainland, while others stood by nervously to see what the aftermath would be. MacGregor invited those who left back, imagining they'd fled in terror and misunderstanding, but no one cared about what he had to say. His own men began deserting after MacGregor forbade looting.

MacGregor claimed the land as the "Republic of the Floridas," uniting East and West in perfect harmony. No one saw his rule as legitimate. Even pirates laughed off his efforts to tax their booty. His presence became increasingly odious when his men went to the mainland, which was technically not covered by the "no looting" orders, and broke into people's homes and took their things.

Amelia was to be the launching point of MacGregor's larger Florida campaign, and he waited for reinforcements that never came. As the situation became more desperate and his funds dried up, he resorted to capturing and selling thirty-one slaves, a move directly contradicting his morals and inciting even more distrust of him from local residents.

MacGregor moved against chief surveyor (and town figurehead) George Clarke, destroying his sawmill and offering money to anyone who captured him or his children. This proved to be a mistake, as Clarke took to reconnoitering Amelia and sending information to Spanish governor José Coppinger. He also helped devise the plan to use McClure's Hill for a counterassault.

To ease the anger against him, MacGregor ordered privateers to leave all non-Spanish vessels alone. He ordered that slaves couldn't be taken from their owners. Alas, it was too late to make amends, and in the effort, he lost his best shot at rushing St. Augustine before it was ready to mount a defense.

Word came that Spain and the Florida militia were gathering to attack MacGregor, who was down to twenty-five soldiers. By this time, he had brought his wife to Amelia. By all accounts, he was in love with the woman, and her safety surely figured into his decision to flee.

With none of the fanfare he'd shown in his initial victory, MacGregor quietly bailed on the scene and left subordinates Ruggles Hubbard and Jared Irwin to clean up. On September 3, he vaguely told his remaining men that he'd been betrayed and would be leaving. The next day, he hopped onto a ship named *Morgiana* and sailed for St. Marys, Georgia. He never repaid his investors and never tried to compensate the families of the men who died.

Vincent Pazos, MacGregor's resident journalist, wrote that the mission's failure wasn't really MacGregor's fault. Pazos blamed the venture's degeneration on some new arrivals who showed up on the island after the battle was over, tried to get a piece of the action, and began instilling their own views. They challenged MacGregor's rigid military discipline, and things quickly started to fall apart.

MacGregor fled the scene for new adventures. In 1821, he carried out one of the most devastating frauds in history, selling Englishmen land in the kingdom of Poyais, which didn't exist. In doing so, he helped trigger the British stock market crash known as the Panic of 1825.

As for Amelia, MacGregor was gone, but the events he'd set in motion were not.

Jared Irwin had successfully repelled the Spanish forces and seemingly cemented himself as king of the Amelia filibusters, but alas, his position was to last only days. Another player was already moving onto the chess board. His name was Louis-Michel Aury, and he was a character every bit as audacious, impressive and deceptive as Gregor MacGregor.

Irwin may have been big-time as a politician in Pennsylvania, but down in Spanish Florida, he was doomed to perpetual relegation as second fiddle to more charismatic figures. Fortunately or unfortunately, that role as second fiddle, too, had a short timeline.

George Clarke and Fernandina Rebuilt Anew

George Clarke was born in St. Augustine while the city was under English rule. When Spain took over in 1783, his family elected to roll the dice and stay with the new authorities. Most people expected Spain to boot them out at best or severely punish them at worst and fled, but the Clarke family remained. The decision would define Clarke's life story.

When Clarke was twelve years old, he started an apprenticeship with Panton, Leslie and Co., who specialized in commerce with Indians. He became an uncommonly competent and effective young man. By the time he was thirty-four, he was a prominent and respected government official, businessman and landowner. Perhaps most interestingly and most importantly, he was also an advocate for Black Americans.

Clarke and Flora: A Romance

Panton, Leslie and Co. used slaves. Clarke fell in love with one named Flora Leslie, whom he met when he was just twelve and she was fifteen. It was no passing crush and proved to have lifelong staying power.

At twenty, Clarke fathered a child with Flora and paid sixty pesos to buy her from the trading firm. They never married, but they stayed together to the end of Flora's days, raising a family of eight children together. One can imagine the scandal this must have been. Not only was the couple mixed race, but they were also unwed. Still, Clarke refused to hide anything about his life, which was all the more impressive considering that he was one of Amelia's most prominent people.

After Flora passed away, Clarke had four more children with another freedwoman, this one named either Anna or Hannah Benet. When Clarke died, he left his entire estate to his children and Benet.

The Reshaping of Amelia

Clarke loved Amelia to his very core. He identified with the place he'd grown up in as an extension of himself. To that end, he wanted the very best for it—and that would start with a redesign. Fernandina had sprung up like something natural growing from the forest. Such a design couldn't long withstand significant growth. They needed a plan that would accommodate expansion.

Clarke took his idea to Governor Enrique White, the man who named Fernandina. White approved. On May 11, 1811, he named Clarke surveyor general and gave him the authority to make the plan a reality.

Being a Spanish colony, Fernandina was bound by legal requirements set forth in the 1573 Law of Indies, which instructed very specific designs for settlements. They were to have sources of good water, fuel and wood; an accessible port for shipping; and arable land. The law dictated that the city be oriented toward a waterfront plaza and that all the streets run parallel and perpendicular to it.

Clarke made the waterfront site the bluff that had played such a large part in the history of the island. The dimensions of residential plots were specified, and orders were given that the outward-facing parts of houses be pleasing to the eye. Clarke drew up a new map to meet the requirements. That was the easy part. Trouble lay in the fact that those boundary lines crossed over and through existing houses. It must have been a chaotic, comical scene: all those people taking the dismantled homes and shanties and rebuilding them, brick by brick, in accord with newly designated plots.

Spain was so absorbed in its war against Napoleon that it couldn't commit resources to Amelia, leaving Clarke alone to do his own thing. He redrew and rebuilt the town, helped freed Blacks secure land grants and, later, helped ensure that they kept their land after ownership of the island switched to the United States in 1821.

During the 1812 Patriot War, Clarke and his brother stood ready to fight the invading "Patriots." When the Amelia Island leadership decided to surrender, Clarke was the one who rowed out in a small boat to offer up their flag. He was one of four men to sign the articles of capitulation.

In 1813, after U.S. troops left, East Florida was a wildland of wayward Patriots determined to resist Spanish rule. Clarke executed a meeting with the malcontents. He got them to agree to accept Spanish authority in exchange for rights to run their own militia, elect their own leaders and operate a magistrate's court.

The agreement split the area into three pieces. Clarke was captain of one of them when Gregor MacGregor attacked in 1817. He led a militia of nearly all Black soldiers to fight the filibuster, but a higher-ranking Spanish officer ordered a retreat. Clarke helped keep the occupiers back from spreading further inland and put his life on the line to stop the transport of enslaved Africans during the MacGregor chaos.

Clarke spied on MacGregor's operation with Spanish forces, looking for weak spots to exploit. It was he who first shared the news that MacGregor had fled the scene. He drew up a plan to take out the remaining enemies there, but Louis Aury showed up before he could.

In 1823, he moved to St. Augustine while it was under U.S. rule. He quit public service for the most part and dedicated himself to his business. He wrote regularly for the *East Florida Herald*. As unbelievable as it seems for a man who did so much in his lifetime, we aren't sure how Clarke died or where he's buried.

Battle of Amelia Island

On September 13, 1817, Spain attempted to wrest control of Amelia Island from MacGregor's forces. MacGregor himself was already long gone, leaving Jared Irwin in charge.

Jared Irwin bet big on MacGregor's victory. A successful politician who'd served in both the Pennsylvania and the U.S. House of Representatives, he packed his bags and headed for the Republic of the Floridas in 1817, ready to claim a commanding role in MacGregor's glorious cause. His decision cemented his place in Amelia's hall of historical misfits.

Irwin joined MacGregor's forces in July. He was put in charge of the Amelia treasury, which was worthless. A couple months later, knowing Spanish forces were gathering against him, MacGregor fled the island and left Irwin in charge. His second-in-command was another late arrival, Ruggles Hubbard, formerly high sheriff of New York City. Both men elected to stay.

One wonders why the men would choose to stake their lives in defense of an island they'd only just arrived at. Perhaps their ambition overshadowed common sense, or perhaps they'd simply gambled too much on the venture and burned too many bridges to back out at that point. After all, they'd effectively shifted national allegiances when they swore fealty to the Republic of the Floridas—regardless of how illegitimate that nation really was. Whatever the case, they mustered defenses while Spanish gathered in St. Augustine.

Spain's forces were put together by José María Coppinger, governor of East Florida from 1816 to 1821. Unable to secure reinforcements from Cuba, Coppinger gathered a force of Florida militia and Black troops. He armed them with artillery and gunboats and prepared an assault.

Spain struck on September 13, 1817. The navy initiated the assault. Land forces followed. Irwin responded.

The two sides traded fire all afternoon, but no one was hurt until Irwin tried to hit the Spanish atop McClure's Hill. His men overshot and instead blasted the camp where Spanish soldiers were staying behind the hill. The volley killed two and injured several others. It took the fight out of the Spanish land forces, who fled.

Coppinger charged the commanding Spanish officer with cowardice. The court found him merely incompetent, enough to remove him from command but not to imprison him—or worse.

Irwin was still in charge when French privateer Louis Aury reached the island on September 17. Irwin initially mustered a show of force but then invited the Frenchman inside. Irwin's motivation seems to have been self-interest rather than fear. He needed the added might and resources that Aury could bring.

Accompanied by an armed guard, Aury immediately began dictating terms. He would only aid Hubbard and Irwin if they agreed to recognize him as the island's supreme commander, not only of the military but of the civil operations as well. Irwin initially argued but quickly caved. The fact was that his own forces were too thin. He needed Aury.

With that, on September 21, 1817, Aury's Mexican revolutionary flag replaced MacGregor's Green Cross.

Aury made Irwin adjutant general. Shortly after, when he decided to legitimize Amelia as a new republic, he made Irwin president—a title that might have been auspicious if only Aury's rule had any substance. Instead, it only added to his disgrace when U.S. forces drove Aury out on December 23, 1817. The occupation ended peacefully, with most of the antagonists sent packing, but Irwin found himself a deserter of his own nation—some would say even a traitor.

Differing accounts exist of Irwin's fate after his Amelia misadventure. Most sources claim he died in the 1818 yellow fever outbreak. *The Historic Splendor of Amelia Island* differs, saying that Joseph Chamberlain, museum researcher, found evidence that Irwin continued to South American with Aury and died on September 20, 1818, after a twelve-day hurricane and typhoid fever epidemic.

McClure's Hill

If you drive up North Fourteenth Street, you'll pass by a historical marker for McClure's Hill. This location was key to the Battle of Amelia Island on September 13, 1817. The hill didn't earn its name from that battle, though.

Zoning records indicate that John McClure "was an Irish adventurer who seems to have come to Fernandina around 1806 or 1807." In 1809, Governor Enrique White granted McClure nine hundred acres.

This good fortune apparently wasn't enough, as McClure proceeded to demand that George Clarke, chief surveyor, grant him the entirety of Fernandina. Fernandina residents sent a petition to White, who promptly refused. The log entry explains that McClure's Hill (there recorded as McClure Hill) was named for John McClure.

On September 13, 1817, Spanish forces rolled artillery to the top of McClure's Hill to bombard Fort San Carlos. George Clarke, who'd had to deal with John McClure over his land stake six years earlier, told the Spanish that the hill would be good for artillery. He wanted to oust Jared Irwin.

Irwin had ninety-four men along with an armed schooner and two privateers. The Spanish fired from gunboats at three thirty in the afternoon. Following the opening shots, McClure's Hill cannons answered with volleys of their own.

Irwin responded with artillery fire from Fort San Carlos. Shells flew throughout the afternoon, but amazingly, not a single person was recorded to have been injured. Bloodshed finally came when Irwin tried to bombard McClure's Hill. His men missed, and the shot hit the Spaniards camped behind the hill. Two men died, others were injured and the Spanish retreated, leaving McClure's Hill to its peace.

For explorers: Less than half a mile north of McClure's Hill is the Bosque Bello cemetery, another hot spot for history lovers and a place covered in this book.

French-Mexican Revolutionary Louis Aury

Few records exist regarding Louis-Michel Aury's childhood. We know that he was born in the 1780s, likely between 1786 and 1788. We also know that he joined the French navy in the early 1800s—a decision that would define the man's life and become the means for him to earn his place, however dubious, in history.

In the navy, he served as a corsair. With the money he made as a privateer, Aury bought his own ship and, eventually, his own fleet, which he used to fight on the side of the Spanish colonies in South America, where multiple nations were rebelling against Spanish rule. Aury had commanded the navy of New Granada for several months in 1813–14 and in 1816 was appointed resident commissioner of Snake Island (now Galveston Island, Texas), which was part of the Republic of Mexico and about halfway through its struggle to win independence from Spain. Aury's crew were called Aury's Patriots, but they were mostly outlaws, thugs and wanderers that he picked up from various ports around the world.

Sketch of Louis Aury. *Amelia Island Museum of History.*

Aury met Gregor MacGregor in South America. Spanish pursuers forced them apart, but during later adventures, Aury got word from fellow revolutionary Pedro Gaul that MacGregor needed help at Amelia. Aury was dealing with a faltering situation at Snake Island, which he'd tried to turn into a lucrative base of operations. His options were drying up, so he set sail once again.

AURY AT AMELIA

Aury entered the Amelia story with a bang. On September 17, 1817, he sailed into harbor in his flagship, the *Mexican Congress*, firing cannons in dramatic greeting. MacGregor had already left town a couple weeks earlier. It's interesting to contemplate how history could have turned in another direction if Aury and MacGregor had combined forces. With the defensive strength of Fort San Carlos, it's conceivable the duo could have established a permanent presence. Alas, MacGregor wasn't there, and his forces had shrunk significantly.

Jared Irwin had already been warned of Aury's approach. He gathered his forces on shore as a show of strength but wasn't really looking for a fight. He invited Aury inside the fort and decided to cast his fate with him.

Irwin tried to negotiate equal terms, but Aury made it clear that either he would be in command, or he would leave the fort to its own devices. The latter option would have left Irwin in charge but with dwindling resources and a small military force. Whether he liked it or not, Irwin needed Aury. Aury demanded that his Mexican Republic banner, which consisted of blue and white checkers bordered by red, replace MacGregor's Green Cross of Florida on September 21.

Under Aury, Amelia became a base for naval assaults on Spanish ships and a port for dealing in contraband slaves. Before September ended (only two weeks after his arrival), his privateers had already dealt in half a million dollars' worth of pirated goods. Within two months, he'd sell over one thousand slaves into Georgia.

Despite these nefarious activities, Aury tried to legitimize Amelia. He brought in the previously mentioned Pedro Gaul, who was a Peruvian lawyer, and Vincent Pazos, a South American journalist. With these intellectuals, he hoped to improve his relations with other world powers.

The presence of Aury's troops stirred up tensions with Irwin's subordinates. A good portion of his crew was composed of Black individuals, and those individuals were accused of stirring up trouble among the slaves already on Amelia. The solution hints at the nature of the "problem," as following a council for arbitration, it was decided that a one-hundred-dollar fine would be imposed on anyone "enticing a slave away from its owner" (according to *MacGregor's Invasion of Florida*, by T. Frederick Davis).

Unbeknownst to the corsair, trouble was floating Aury's way. Several British officers had been on a mission to the Bahamas. When that endeavor went awry, they changed course for Amelia, where they hoped to join MacGregor. On discovering the Highlander already gone, some officers left, but others decided to attempt overthrowing Aury.

Aury was having none of the Brit rebellion. He anchored five of his privateers at harbor and unmasked their cannons, all trained on Fernandina. With that, he declared martial law for ten days. He put together a kangaroo court to try one of the officers as a show of force and a deterrent to future rebellion. He built a jury of his scrupulous subordinates, planning to deliver a guilty verdict that would allow him to conduct a very public execution.

Things didn't go his way, though, as someone managed to reach St. Marys, Georgia, where stayed one of the officers who'd left upon finding that MacGregor was gone. The officer was a skilled lawyer. He presented his defense, closing with a threat to reveal Aury and crew's illegal proceeds to the nations of which they were still citizens. This was enough to win the officer's freedom.

Aury continued increasing the profitability of Fernandina's port, largely through the slave trade. He made good with the soldiers of Florida's Northern Division by sharing profits with them, thereby buttering up a key potential opponent. He waged mental warfare by threatening to rouse every slave in the area to rebellion if he was attacked. The goods flowing into Fernandina included fine Spanish cigars, silk, spices, coffee and sugar.

Aury wanted to further legitimize the place, so he held elections. Irwin was voted president. Madcap as the start of the whole thing was, revolting as was its trade in slaves, Aury actually seemed on the cusp of making Amelia a legitimate political institution.

Then in came news that kindled disbelief and fury in Aury. The United States government had been observing his exploits, and it wasn't happy.

Aury's Defeat

Aury had assumed that the United States would at least support his effort to liberate Amelia from Spain, if not give him full-blown support. Reality proved much different.

In December, in the midst of Aury's seeming victory, the corsair received word that the United States was preparing to move on Amelia. Aury was outraged and ready to scrap. His mood quickly changed as the reality of the situation became clear. He was no coward, but battling the United States would be suicide.

Back in the United States, discussions had begun two months earlier. On October 31, President James Monroe made the call to move on Aury. The decision didn't come easily. Many objected to interfering in the "Amelia Island situation," including Henry Clay. Supporters, however, understood the potential strategic gains. Taking Amelia from Aury would show the world that Spain was inept and incapable of properly defending its American territories.

Monroe officially announced the action during his annual message, delivered on December 2. He was going to retake Amelia, which he called a "festering fleshpot"—a *fleshpot* being a place of hedonism. Ultimately, his justification was a January 15, 1811 law that prohibited foreign powers from occupying Florida. There was also Aury's illegal slave trade to think about.

Furthermore, the United States was in negotiations with Spain for the cession of the Florida territories, and Aury threatened that. The United States sent Aury an official notice to vacate, notifying him, "Should you, contrary to the expectations of the President of the United States, refuse to give us peaceable possession of the island, the consequence of resistance must rest with you."

Aury didn't have the forces to fend off a full-blown assault, so he prepared to flee. As military resistance was futile, his man Pazos and others prepared to challenge the United States in court. To that end, they went about preparing a legal defense.

On December 23, 1817, U.S. forces landed on Amelia's beaches. When the first boat made landfall, Aury fired blanks from his cannons. Ostensibly, it was a show of surrender, but surely Aury enjoyed startling the enemy.

Troops marched into Amelia whistling "Yankee Doodle." They raised the U.S. flag on that day, which would be the last time Amelia had to live through a military transition.

Aury left, but he had to sell his flagship to repay his debts and was forced to hang around St. Marys for months while his ships were repaired. This must have been dreadful for his ego, as people harassed and mocked him every chance they got. Eventually, in March, he left for a new adventure in the Isthmus of Panama.

Aury and Pazos would continue arguing legally for some time, but the die had been cast. Simón Bolívar, the lead revolutionary against Spanish rule of Latin America, sided with the United States on the Aury situation and denounced the actions of his former subordinate, further hurting Aury's chances of persuasion.

Many opposed Monroe's actions, and he had to defend himself for months afterward. Notably, Spanish envoy to the United States Louis-Michel de Onis challenged the legality of the occupation. Monroe's case continued to be that Aury was using the island as a base for illegal and immoral activities, that the 1811 law still held sway and that Aury threatened to disrupt land negotiations with Spain. He didn't win, but he drew many sympathetic supporters.

An 1820 newspaper reported Aury was operating near Cuba, but he faded from history after that point. A document dated August 20, 1821, mentioned Aury's death, which might have resulted from being thrown by a horse.

The Omni Amelia Island Resort named Aury Island after the privateer.

In the old Fort San Carlos parade ground in Old Town Fernandina stands a marker commemorating the African slaves that Aury brought to Amelia.

AMELIA UNDER BRITAIN

Two Treaties of Paris bookended England's twenty-year reign over Amelia.

The English took control of Florida with the signing of the 1763 Treaty of Paris, which ended the Seven Years' War and redistributed lands between Great Britain, Portugal, France and Spain. The English booted three-thousand-plus Spanish residents from Florida and cut the state down the middle into West and East Florida, their fourteenth and fifteenth colonies.

Under its new rulers, Amelia would no longer be a haven for escaped slaves and Indians. It would be reshaped largely through slave labor as it became a major exporter of indigo. Britain ran Amelia throughout the Revolutionary War and lost ownership of it with the 1783 Treaty of Paris, which decided terms ending the Revolutionary War.

With that, almost exactly twenty years after one Paris Treaty put Amelia in its hands, another Paris Treaty took it away.

GOVERNOR JAMES MOORE AND THE ENGLISH ATTACK

By 1700, troublesome Ensign Diego de Jean was gone from the Amelia mission. Roughly two hundred Indians lived there with Spanish priests and soldiers. In José de Zúñiga y Cerda, they had an engaged governor. The food situation had vastly improved, and relations between Spaniards and Englishmen were calm, with Spanish residents along the coast expected to assist shipwrecked English travelers that happened their way. In other words, things seemed very much on the up-and-up.

Yet events back in Europe were cranking up global tensions. Things would soon boil over and end the Santa Catalina mission forever.

John Moore served in various political posts starting in 1677 and came to lead a group called the Goose Creek Men, which formed in Goose Creek, South Carolina. They were an odd mix of farmers, tradesmen and White servants who'd fulfilled the requirements of their indentured servitude and earned their freedom. In 1670, they all moved to the Province of Carolina, which included the lands that today make up both Carolinas, Georgia, Tennessee, Alabama, Mississippi and a sliver of Florida. By the time the 1700 gubernatorial elections rolled around, they were a powerful force in regional politics.

The election that Moore won was highly controversial, but protestations by rival Dissenters amounted to nothing. Legitimate election or not, Moore took his seat as governor and immediately began leading raids into Spanish Florida.

Moore's legacy is generally a dubious one, but his concerns regarding Florida were legitimate. French territory bordered Carolina to the west, which would mean a precarious position with a second enemy in Spain to the south. Moore's concerns mounted in 1702 with the outbreak of Queen Anne's War—the American theater of the War of Spanish Succession. Spain's king had died without an heir, and European powers battled for the crown. The alliances that emerged lent additional weight to Moore's concerns about France and Spain allying against him.

Moore took the initiative. Using money granted him by the colonial government, he led fourteen ships and about eight hundred men (five hundred colonists and three to four hundred Indians, mostly Yamasee) against Spanish Florida. Moore directed the sea forces while Colonel Robert Daniel led ground troops.

Amelia, then called Santa Maria, never really stood a chance. They hadn't yet completed their fortifications. The Crown had sent funds for a watchtower, but the governor diverted them to building a St. Augustine seawall.

Juan Tejada and Domingo Gonzsales were sentries on the night of Moore's attack. Without proper fortifications, they weren't guards so much as targets. Daniel's forces snuck up the side of the bluff and took the men out. The islanders were alerted to their presence soon after.

Residents scattered. Fathers Domingo Santos and Manuel de Urissa frantically rang church bells to call residents into the mission. The people rallied to the sound, heard news of the siege and jetted for the mainland. Nice thought by Santos and Urissa, but everyone knew the mission couldn't protect them. As if punctuating that insight, flaming arrows thudded into the mission roof.

Daniel and his troops followed the sound of bells. Once the church was within sight, Yamasee archers launched arrows with burning moss wrapped around them. The mission was soon engulfed in flames.

Captain Francisco Fuentes de Galarza, head of the mission garrison, managed to get word to St. Augustine. Governor Zúñiga had insufficient men and time to match Moore's forces on the battleground, so he had everyone cram into the Castillo de San Marco in St. Augustine, which still stands as the oldest masonry fort in the country.

St. Augustine burned that night, but the fort held.

Moore's forces laid waste to the Spanish mission system, but the repulsion at the *castillo* rendered the victories moot. His enterprise was considered a failure and a waste of resources. Moore resigned his post in disgrace.

In 1704, Moore reentered Florida history when he led forces against the Apalachee Indians, allies of Spain. Moore's forces crushed the Apalachee and led to their disintegration. Moore died in 1706 from a tropical disease.

We Are the Egmont Isle, Coo Coo Ca Choo

A few twists of fate and we might be calling Amelia by the less sonorous name "Egmont Isle" today.

In 1748, British politician John Perceval took over as second Earl of Egmont in the Peerage of Ireland. Later appointed first lord of the Admiralty, he received sixty-five thousand acres of land in northeast Florida, which he put to productive use at Mount Royal, near the St. Johns River. Governor James Grant appreciated Perceval's ambition and gave him another ten thousand acres, this on the island we know as Amelia today.

Perceval wanted to use the Amelia River to transport plantation crops out into Cumberland Sound and off to England. To accomplish his goal, he reasoned that each landowner should get a plot of Egmont Isle on which to build a warehouse to store goods for transport. In 1770, ten slaves were dispatched to clear the land for this purpose. Egmont Isle was nearly finalized, but John Perceval died in December.

Perceval was gone and with him the name Egmont. Yet his vision wouldn't die. The executors of his will brought the center of his operations from Mount Royal to Amelia. With that, the island that had been a Spanish oasis from slavery became a place of English slave labor.

With Perceval's passing came the arrival of one of Amelia's most intriguing characters: Stephen Egan.

A Gray Season

Moore's campaign didn't end Spain's rule over Amelia, but it significantly diminished Spain's power in the area, creating a power vacuum into which chaos poured. The Carolina-Florida border became a wild hinterland of roving bandits, slavers and malcontents.

Circumstances encouraged lawlessness among decent people. As part of their war efforts, England and Spain forbade their respective colonies from trading with their enemies in the opposing colonies. This made sense from the seat of a throne across the sea, but for the residents actually on the ground, it was unrealistic and made life impossible. Each side had abundant resources that the other side lacked.

So English and Spanish colonists alike simply ignored the orders. Spanish Florida governor Francisco del Moral y Sánchez? let the illegal trade happen without taking any measures to stop it or even report it to the Crown. He understood the reality of the situation.

From Moore's 1702 razing to England's 1763 adoption of Amelia, the island hung suspended in this uncertain, transitory world. Spain technically owned the land, but England steered its development. This gray period between empires could only be achieved through the efforts of a truly epic squatter. Luckily, in James Oglethorpe, England had one.

James Oglethorpe: Best Damn Squatter in U.S. History

James Edward Oglethorpe was a member of the English parliament, the founder of Georgia, a social reformer and perhaps the greatest squatter in world history. He's the man who gave Amelia its name, but he contributed more than that to the place's strange, snaking history.

Oglethorpe was born in England in 1696. He was a military man and politician of some distinction, but he comes to our story primarily through his work as a social reformer.

In 1700s England, debtors' prisons were common. As the name suggests, these were jails where people were sent when they couldn't pay their bills. After one of his friends died in such a prison, Oglethorpe decided to investigate the national institution of debtors' prisons. Returning with scathing reports of mistreatment, Oglethorpe spent years fighting for change that he never quite won. He began looking elsewhere to enact his reforms—namely, to America.

Oglethorpe took control of the province of Georgia, England's thirteenth colony, on April 21, 1732. He wanted to build a society where debtors from England could get a second start in life. The future Peach State morphed into something else, but that's another story for another book. For our purposes, we pick up Oglethorpe's tale while he was exploring his lands in March 1736 and stumbled on enchanting Amelia Island. Immediately, he set himself to gaining control of the island.

One problem stood in his way—he was English, and Amelia still belonged to Spain. Oglethorpe wasn't a man to be deterred by such minor inconveniences. He met with Governor Francisco del Moral y Sánchez and negotiated terms. He offered to remove his men from Fort George Island in exchange for Amelia. Sánchez agreed.

What makes the story so comical is that Sánchez didn't have the time (or, perhaps, inclination) to check with the Spanish crown. He just went ahead and did it. This meant that the transfer of authority wasn't really official, but Oglethorpe moved on anyway. He wasted no time getting to work, knowing the Spanish crown could have any range of reactions once it heard of his move.

Charmed by the island's picturesque beauty, Oglethorpe nevertheless had a practical purpose for Amelia. It was to be England's southernmost buffer against the Spanish, and he armed it for that purpose. With him he brought sixteen Highlander families consisting of forty people. He knew there was a chance that the Spanish crown wouldn't take kindly to his presence, and he had fortifications hastily built while the Highlanders planted food and constructed shelters.

Oglethorpe's squatters held the land for six years. Then, in April 1737, thirty Spaniards rode up on shore. When sixteen of the new arrivals approached the fort, Oglethorpe's men opened fire.

The Spanish attempted to excuse their presence as an innocent stopover, but the English were having none of it and drove them from the island. Oglethorpe operated under the assumption that Spain's purpose had been to test their defenses. He expected a return.

In 1738, Oglethorpe began preparing for war. Trouble was in the air. He built up his navy and ground forces with his own money and granted permission for pirates to attack Spain's vessels. On September 7, 1739, he paid Creek Indians to harass Spaniards. A month later, the War of Jenkins' Ear broke out. A contest between Spain and Britian focused mostly on the waters of Central and South America, it spilled over into areas all over the world, including Amelia.

With the outbreak of war, the Spanish returned to Amelia in November. This time, they successfully snuck up Amelia's bluff and took out two Highlanders.

Oglethorpe responded with two hundred men, cutting a swath south toward St. Augustine before being stopped at the very same Castillo de San

Marcos that had fended off Governor James Moore in 1702. His campaign wasn't considered a failure entirely, as he caused significant losses to the enemy, but it was far from total victory.

In 1742, Spanish warships massed outside Amelia Island. Oglethorpe wanted to dig in his heels, but Britain ordered him to stand down. He drew his forces off Amelia. Oglethorpe did so, returning to Georgia and exiting our story. He regained some military clout when he defeated a Spanish counter-invasion at the Battle of Bloody Marsh on St. Simons Island, Georgia.

Egan's Indigo

Starting up a new town in harsh country requires exceptional leaders, and exceptional leaders are hard to find. Luckily, Perceval's widow, Lady Egmont, knew of such a man. Irishman Stephen Egan established a solid reputation through his successful run as superintendent of an Irish estate Egmont owned.

Egan's task at Amelia would be a difficult one. Not only was he being asked to stand up a brand new commercial enterprise, but he was also being asked to successfully cultivate indigo, which is notoriously difficult to grow and even more difficult to process.

Egan was up to the job. Allowing himself no excuses, he committed himself to learning the art of indigo through books. He brought his wife, three sons, servants and horses to a plantation on Amelia's north end.

His enterprise was a success by any measure. Near the town bluff, he built warehouses. In 1774, they held 2,095 pounds of indigo, with each pound sold to England for four shillings and sixpence.

More importantly than his success as a businessman, Egan's legacy is marked by his treatment of his slaves. Here we enter the always sticky and ever controversial area of moral relativism, but however one feels about it, Egan treated his laborers far better than custom expected. He treated them like employees rather than slaves, showing respect in his interactions with them and ensuring the workers had the resources to learn business, carpentry, farming and animal husbandry. He built villages for his workforce and made sure that each man had a wife.

Of course, Egan's work journals also make clear that his benevolent treatment was at least partially inspired by shrewdness. He understood that happy workers produce more than unhappy workers. The ultimate morality

Drawing of James Oglethorpe. *Amelia Island Museum of History.*

or immorality of his legacy is for readers to contemplate.

Egan's enterprise attracted other would-be planters, but they were quickly deterred by Georgian raiders that swooped in from the wilds to snatch money and slaves. Egan himself wasn't immune to the raiders' harassment. In August 1776, he asked for help from Governor Patrick Tonyn, who responded with a three-hundred-man force dubbed the Rangers. It's believed that Daniel McGirt, who had become a Loyalist raider that terrorized north Florida, learned his trade while serving in the Rangers.

The Night They Burned Ol' Fernandina Down

The Rangers proved insufficient protection on May 18, 1777, when Continental soldiers stormed Amelia. Led by Colonel Samuel Elbert, the force landed on the island's shores and wasted no time with negotiations. Lieutenant Ward led a patrol to the south end of the island. Before he reached the southern shore, British troops opened fire, killing Ward and two of his men.

Elbert was unamused by the British volley and sent twenty men inland to burn every house to the ground.

Egan led the retreat of his family and one hundred slaves. They made it to the mainland and pushed through forests to reach St. Augustine and the protection of the British army. They moved to an unfinished estate, which they built up and named Cecilton Plantation (the historic site can be visited today).

By the time Elbert's men were done, a smoky haze filled harbor and woods alike.

Egan rebuilt his business, but he did so on the mainland along the St. Johns River and never returned to Amelia. His name is memorialized by Egan's Creek and Egan's Creek Park at the corner of North Wolff Street and Atlantic Avenue. There, a historical marker summarizes his story.

1794: Une Parenthèse à la Française (A French Interlude)

Over two hundred years after Pedro Menéndez massacred Jean Ribault at Matanzas Inlet, the French flag flew again over Amelia—albeit only briefly.

In 1793, still possessed by the energy of the French Revolution and successfully overthrowing their own monarchy, the French were hungry for more powers to topple. Spain seemed as good a target as any. In March 1793, the powers went to war.

Edmond Charles Genet was French minister to the United States. He knew that the area around Amelia was a no-man's-land, with wanderers of various loyalties or no loyalty at all mingling along the shores. They were men comfortable with violence and hardship—in short, men primed to become revolutionaries.

Florida governor Juan Nepomuceno de Quesada y Barnuevo Arrocha guessed that Amelia would be an early target in the conflict. He further assessed the island was too vulnerable to protect, withdrew all troops and weapons from it and ordered residents to evacuate. He instructed them set their homes and shops on fire. He had to think of the larger strategy for Spanish Florida, and indefensible Amelia was a pawn worth sacrificing.

It must have been difficult for residents to destroy everything they'd built, especially without an immediate threat before them, but Nepomuceno was proved correct. Three months later, a French warship named *Las Casas* approached Amelia. Finding the place abandoned, soldiers stayed behind with a small armory. So it was that, in April 1795, a French flag flew again over Amelia, which was to be the headquarters of a revolution against Spanish control of the United States.

It wouldn't fly long.

On August 2, 1795, Spain responded with soldiers aboard a schooner, two gunboats and two brigs. Three of the ships grounded themselves on approaching the bluff. The resulting delay gave the French time to escape into Georgia. It was something of an embarrassing offensive for Spain, but sufficient to drive France off Amelia.

Spain and France signed a treaty shortly thereafter. The victory must have seemed thin to Amelia's residents as they returned to cindered houses to rebuild. Still, many resolved to start anew. Amelia isn't a place that people leave easily.

Patriot War of East Florida

General George Mathews is one of those guys that just jumps out of history books. He enters our tale at five foot four and seventy-two years old, known to dress in ruffled shirts with knee britches and high-topped boots. To this fashion he added a three-cornered hat and Revolutionary War sword.

Mathews started life as a farmer and merchant and went on to become a colonel in the colonial militia, playing a major role in the Battle of Point Pleasant, West Virgnia. He served as a colonel of the Ninth Virginia Regiment in the Revolutionary War and was captured in the Battle of Germantown, spending four years as a prisoner of war and then living on parole in New York.

His entry into our tale comes in November 1810. Spanish Florida governor Vicente Folch was trying to keep his region together at a time when the Napoleonic Wars had stretched Spain so thin that it couldn't commit enough forces to keep its American colonies safe and viable. The situation had become so dire that Folch was considering giving the land up. Word of this got to Mathews, who took the message to President James Madison.

Madison elected to try his hand at taking both East and West Florida at once. From here, the story gets slippery. Madison directed Mathews to incite a revolution in the Spanish colonies. His commands were vague—a fact that would play significantly into what followed.

Mathews traveled to St. Marys, Georgia, and began reconnoitering northern Florida, with a plan to sack St. Augustine. While he did his spying, he wrote vociferously to Secretary of State James Monroe. Monroe initially replied with encouragement, but over time, his responses slowed and finally stopped completely. This fact has been a bone of contention among historians for centuries.

One side of the debate contends that Madison was silent in order to keep himself from being culpable while secretly supporting Mathews in all he would come to do. The other side contends that Madison's administration followed a policy of nonresponse implicitly meaning nonsupport. Whichever is true, Mathews wasn't a man who backed out easily. He never heard an explicit "cease and desist," so he kept going. The full debate has too many participants and nuances for the purposes of this book, but the author encourages history lovers to dig into it—it's fascinating stuff.

Mathews lacked the numbers to take St. Augustine, so he set his sights on Amelia Island.

General George Mathews' Patriot Flag. *Amelia Island Museum of History.*

His plans were leaked, at which time Spain wrote to Monroe and President James Madison asking them to denounce the whole affair. Monroe refused to do so. Instead, he laid out a case for the United States being justified in taking control of East Florida, partially because Spain owed the United States money and partially because Spain had failed in its duty to protect its citizens in Florida. This wasn't an explicit endorsement of military occupation but rather a defense of the general notion of the virtues of U.S. control. He kept enough wiggle room to maintain plausible deniability.

It was understood that Spain's control over Florida was so weak that England could likely snatch it from them rather easily. That would mean one of the United States' enemies had a foothold in its territory. This was unacceptable to Monroe and Madison.

Mathews took Monroe's response as backing for his continued plan. He'd been slowly signing on those few people in the area who cared enough to fight to take Amelia from Spain, but his forces were thin. He eventually got together around 125 men. He also thought he'd be able to count on 75 U.S. troops deserting their posts and joining him, but that fell apart at the last minute.

He did, however, manage to enlist Commodore Hugh Campbell, who had five gunboats to offer. Campbell wasn't all onboard. He wanted official word from up north but agreed to make the advance with Mathews until that word came.

Mathews led his Patriots into Florida on March 13, 1912. As he cut a swath through northern Florida, men left their stations to join him, until his force swelled to about 250 men. As this was going on, the people of Fernandina were preparing their defense. They'd gotten word that Mathews was coming.

The people of Fernandina put together a good defensive force, but when Mathews arrived, they elected to negotiate. Commodore Campbell had serious misgivings about the whole affair, but he said nothing about it while they parleyed, so the Spanish had no idea that the man wasn't fully invested. Without Campbell, Mathews's forces likely would have been insufficient to take the island. Ignorant of the commodore's secret feelings, the Fernandinans only knew that Mathews had five gunboats with cannons trained on Amelia.

In the end, Don Justo Lopez, commandant of Fernandina's Spanish military, surrendered. As has happened so many times over Amelia's history, the island switched hands during a militant exchange that involved little to no violence. With that, yet another flag was hoisted over Amelia Island.

Yet the assault wasn't the end of the matter. The affair created an international scandal, with Spain denouncing the illegal occupation. Afraid of inciting war, Madison played dumb and swore off the event. He relieved Mathews of his duties and publicly denounced the man.

Mathews, who'd served with absolute loyalty for most of his life, was enraged. He promised to go to Washington, D.C., and reveal the dark secrets behind the whole event. Before he could, though, he died. It was August 1812.

REVOLUTIONARY WAR AMELIA

England owned Florida through the Revolutionary War (1775–83). The English separated the state into West and East Florida, their fourteenth and fifteenth colonies. So Florida was out of Spanish hands and fair game for the Revolutionary conflict, yet it's mostly left out of discussions about the war.

A multitude of factors likely led to the quietude around the subject. Florida was underpopulated, undeveloped and far from the main areas of conflict. Some historians have suggested that Florida's later alliance with the Confederacy during the Civil War led to its being unofficially blackballed from full coverage, as the northern winners were the ones who got to write early American history.

Whatever the case, Florida is often left out of Revolutionary War discussions. The state did see action, though, in the Battles of Alligator Creek Bridge, New Smyrna, Thomas Creek and Amelia Island. Additionally, Georgian patriots harassed and attacked loyalist Floridians, including Stephen Egan and Amelia's residents.

Amelia's new English residents were energized by the challenge of building a new world, intent on contributing to colonial efforts. Many were funded by English grants to clear land and build settlements. They mostly viewed England as a fair employer and, being newer to colonial rule than northern states, hadn't had time to develop resentments. So passionate was their loyalty that they burned effigies of John Hancock and Samuel Adams after the war was declared. East Florida governor Patrick Tonyn announced that British loyalists would find a welcoming haven in his territory.

Amelia's day of conflict came on May 18, 1777, when Colonel Elbert led Continental forces against them. He landed beneath the island's bluff and ordered Lieutenant Ward to lead a patrol to the south end. Before the men reached their destination, British troops opened fire, killing Ward and two of his men.

Elbert ordered his men to burn every house on Amelia. Four days later, the English Amelia that had been so painstakingly built atop the bones of Spanish Amelia was in cinders. The island remained largely uninhabited until the Treaty of Paris, which ended the Revolutionary War and returned Amelia to Spain in 1783.

England never again laid claim to the island.

CONFEDERATE SWAN SONG

It was more of a picnic than a bivouac and more of a party than a battle, but on January 8, 1861, the Confederacy overran Fernandina, two days before Florida officially seceded from the Union. Fort Clinch had been abandoned except for an engineer and some staff. The Confederates just walked right in.

The occupying force was the Third Regiment of Florida Volunteers, led by Colonel William Scott Dilworth. The Volunteers were composed of everyday people rather than professional soldiers. They were bolstered by the Fernandina Volunteers led by Joseph Finegan, whose repossessed mansion was turned into an orphanage by Chloe Merrick.

The Confederacy hadn't completed its flag yet, so on January 13, Dilworth hoisted one that looked similar to the U.S. flag except that it had a single star in the upper left field, identical to the design used for the old Texas naval flag. A month later, the Confederate flag was completed and hoisted in place of the makeshift one.

Over the next months, Confederate blockade runners hid out in Fernandina. Its uses otherwise were limited. General Lee ordered the spot abandoned in March 1862.

Lee's thought process in abandoning the island isn't clear. He visited it twice, the first time noting serious concern about the fort's defensibility. On a second trip, though, he seemed more optimistic, despite noting the lack of motivation among the Fernandina Volunteers. "It is difficult to get our people to realize their position," he wrote to his daughter (as documented in Jaccard's *Historic Splendor of Amelia Island*).

Despite his uptick in confidence, Lee still pulled the troops out. When word of the Union advance came, he instructed the people to flee or fight for themselves. Citizens initially vowed to make a stand. They set up defenses. Some fired on the approaching gunships. But as the full scale of the invasion slowly presented itself, people started to come to their senses.

They ran, hoping that their decision to do so hadn't come too late.

The Train That Exploded

A train roared and lurched forward on its rails as Union gunships began firing on Fernandina. The land forces wouldn't be far away. Most of the townspeople had already fled, but some stragglers remained. One of them was Senator David E. Yulee.

Yulee had waited until shots were cracking around him to make his move and now watched in horror as the train departed. He took off at a dead sprint, brought himself in line with a car, leapt and grabbed hold. He climbed inside and took a seat near James Broome, minister Archibald Baker and Joseph Finegan.

Musket and cannon shot split the air. Yulee and friends laughed nervously as they felt the train gather speed. Amazingly, they had escaped—or so they thought.

Two men in the rear of the train felt similarly relieved. They sat on a sofa atop a car that had been packed with furniture. They were waving handkerchiefs in goodbye to Fernandina as a shell from the Union's *Ottawa* gunboat blasted their car, and them, to bits.

The brakeman managed to unhook the destroyed car, and the rest of the train escaped. Yet Fernandina had been overtaken once again.

Dupont Cometh

Commodore Samuel Dupont led Union forces onto Fernandina on March 3–4. He met little resistance but made sure to crush that which did appear. His USS *Ottawa* gunboat took out the doomed furniture riders from Yulee's train and commandeered the *Darlington* steamship as it tried to escape, full of women, children and military supplies.

Soldiers of the Fourth New Hampshire, Ninth Maine, and Ninety-Seventh Pennsylvania sacked the town. They destroyed and stole property, despite orders from the provost marshal to block any shipments of stolen goods sent back north. Some got drunk and terrorized the few citizens who remained.

Dupont's assessment of Fort Clinch was very different from Lee's. He felt that it could have repelled his forces if it had been manned—not that it really mattered by that point. The battle, such as it was, was over. Amelia was now Union territory.

Under its new authority, Amelia reverted to a role it had played during its Spanish years, acting as a sanctuary for runaway slaves. So much so that, by 1863, 1,200 Black residents called it home alongside 200 Whites.

Yulee's Dream: The Florida Railroad

The Amelia Island Welcome Center used to be a train depot at the terminus of the first Florida Railroad, the longest Florida railroad completed before the Civil War kicked off. Standing in front of the center is a statue of Senator David Yulee, who contributed more than any other person to building the railroad and northeastern Florida. He was fairly obsessed with creating the project. Despite years of setbacks and frustration, his eyes remained fixed on making Fernandina the "Newport of the South."

The Florida Railroad helped shape Fernandina. What is now Old Town Fernandina wouldn't suit the railroad because of the marshes. Not wanting to get left behind, the entire town moved one mile up to the railroad.

Yulee started construction in 1855. The partially completed route went into service in 1858, connecting Fernandina to Starke. The Panic of 1857 slowed things down as Yulee had to find new means to fund the project. He did so by joining forces with northern investors led by Edward Dickerson. They demanded to be majority stockholders, wresting control from Yulee. The railroad reached completion in 1861 when it reached Cedar Key.

Florida Transit Company stock certificate. *State Library and Archives of Florida.*

The train connected commerce from northeastern Florida shores to northwestern. Previously, ships had to travel south all the way around Florida. The route was dangerous, and many craft went down on the way.

The railroad survived the war on shaky legs. All the damage it took was expensive and difficult to repair. It was nearly taken offline permanently but was saved. It's gone through many hands since then. It's still active, though shortened. Named the First Coast Railroad, it connects Yulee eastward to Fernandina Beach and northward to Seals, Georgia.

Amelia Island, United States of America

With that, Amelia Island finally saw its last change of flags. Since March 3, 1862, it's been held by the United States of America.

Chapter 8

Chloe Merrick and the Civil War Orphanage That Was a Mansion

Chloe Merrick wasn't born in Florida, but she left a mark on that state that few could compete with. If Fernandina Beach were ever to put together a Hall of Heroes, she'd be in it.

Merrick was born on April 18, 1832, to Sylvanus and Achsah Pollard Merrick. The family lived near Syracuse, New York. At the time she was born, her brothers were aged twenty and seventeen, while her sister was three.

Merrick lost her mother in childhood. Sometime around 1837, the family moved to Syracuse, and it was in that city that Merrick earned her chops as a public school teacher. She'd spend most of her life as an educator, but her true passion was the abolitionist movement that sought freedom and fair treatment for African Americans.

Merrick was a pretty woman and came from a good family, so she could have lived an easier life than the one she chose. She just wasn't the kind of person to take the easy way out of things. Driven by a fierce will toward justice and decency, she spent most of her life helping Black Americans. Rather than stoop to silk bedsheets, she endured frequent financial instability and physical hardship in order to perform her ethical duties as she saw them.

Merrick in Fernandina

In 1862, Merrick and Cornelia Smith volunteered to go to Fernandina to educate freed slaves. At that time, Amelia was home to roughly 1,200

Portrait of Chloe Merrick. *Amelia Island Museum of History.*

Black citizens, mostly former slaves, and 200 Whites. The Civil War had torn families and communities apart, casting orphans to the wind. It wasn't the Black children alone—it was everybody. Chloe found them everywhere, like windblown bits of Spanish moss. One group of homeless children was suffering through smallpox in a place she described as "jail-like." Another child was enslaved by an old freed Black woman.

Other problems abounded. During the Civil War, some Union soldiers seduced Black women and then returned to their northern homes (or were killed in battle), leaving behind pregnant women or women with newborn children—in both cases, women with kids and no support. One such woman was named Sarah. Of her, Merrick wrote that "the mother [was] left to bear alone the burden of caring for the off-spring whose natural guardians have left the South, and these helpless ones to wear away a weary life, looking in vain for their seducer's promised return."

Merrick witnessed conditions of such deprivation that she knew education wasn't going to be enough. The people needed basic amenities, shelter and food. Never a woman to sit back and hope someone else would take care of things, Merrick jumped right in and solved the problem herself. Her challenge lay in securing the funds to get all the orphans into shelter.

"I am not sufficient, alone, to meet and bring order out of the chaotic elements surrounding me," she wrote to a Syracuse associate. "I need the earnest sympathy, aid, wise council and prayers of all those whose hearts are with me in this. It seems to me that a kind Providence had led hitherto, and I assure you I still earnestly desire to have this work so directed that it shall meet the approval of our Common Father."

Her quest eventually sent her back to Syracuse, where she had connections to the upper crust of society. She raised money for her project. Saxton, the general who'd originally sought her help, gave $300 and a large quantity of supplies such as clothing and tools.

When Merrick returned to Fernandina, she did so with the resources she needed. Next up, she needed a suitable location. Fortunately, the same circumstances that had produced so many orphans also bore up a suitable building.

Finegan's House

The answer to Merrick's prayers came in the form of a mansion.

In 1863, the establishment of Florida's Direct Tax Commission meant that properties owned by Confederates who didn't pay their taxes would be seized and sold or leased out. One such house belonged to Irish immigrant Joseph Finegan.

In the 1850s, Finegan had been a partner in David Yulee's Florida Railroad (he named one of his children Yulee Finegan). His construction company built the rail portion that ran through Fernandina. He was an accomplished man, working as a lawyer and lumber mill operator, among other ventures. He had a mansion built between Eleventh and Twelfth Streets but never lived in it. Before Finegan could occupy his house, Florida seceded from the Union and the Civil War began.

Finegan dropped everything to fight with the Confederates. He attained the rank of brigadier general. In 1860, he organized a militia group named the Fernandina Volunteers. They helped occupy Amelia's Fort Clinch in 1861.

While serving in the war, Finegan was unable to pay his taxes, which meant that his mansion became eligible for purchase. Merrick swooped in and bought it up. There were already some dispossessed individuals squatting in the residence. It's possible they were Finegan's former slaves.

Eighteen acres of estate surrounded Finegan's house. Its vast size was good in the sense that it had plenty of room for Merrick's charges, but unfortunate in that the grounds required a tremendous amount of upkeep.

In 1865, Merrick housed up to seventy orphans in Finegan's house. Her success took her to new levels of reputation and attracted other teachers and nurses (it's possible that Harriet Tubman helped for a bit), but it had its drawbacks. Increasing numbers of people showed up at the door looking for a place to stay. Merrick had twenty-six children in her care in February 1865. By July, the number had climbed to thirty. Before the year passed, there were fifty. Merrick strained herself physically and mentally to keep up with it all.

Food for the children was limited. They ate mostly military rations bolstered by harvests from gardens that they planted. One frightening stretch saw the rations suspended. Only an unexpected grant saved them. The situation hung on by a permanently frayed shoestring.

Merrick's health was at risk. She was overworked on all levels, and malaria was still a serious threat in Florida. She personally knew teachers who had been struck down by the disease. In addition to the obvious stresses of running the orphanage, she had to worry about the rumored repeal of the tax law that enabled her to buy Finegan's home. She was also bothered by the soldiers returning from the Civil War. They harassed her and showed a shockingly brutal streak of racism.

The events tested Merrick's faith. She wrote, "God, what lessons art thou teaching the nation in this scourge thou art permitting thus to visit this oppressed people?"

Yet, through it all, she persevered.

As the smoke from the Civil War cleared and Reconstruction began, the nation tried heal wounds and achieve some level of unity. In this spirit, the federal government changed its stance on the repossession of homes from Confederate soldiers. The Finegan house was returned to the estate of its original owner. The orphans were put into apprenticeships or sent to freedmen's institutions.

Merrick met Harrison Reed, tax commissioner of Florida, in 1863. Six years later, they married in Syracuse. The two contributed civically for the rest of their lives. Merrick passed away in 1897.

Finegan eventually sold the house to pay off debts. It became St. Mary's Priory, which no longer exists. No construction remains on the plot. When Union forces overran Fernandina in 1862, an officer went through Finegan's house and found a high-quality Bible, quality books and other items.

A former residence of Merrick's can be seen in Fernandina. It's one of the last pre–Civil War houses left on Amelia. After Merrick, the owner of a trolley and an ice plant named John Simmons bought it. Today, it's known as the Merrick-Simmons House. You can see it at 102 South Tenth Street.

Chapter 9

Extra! Extra! The First Newspaper on Amelia Island

The *News-Leader*, based in Fernandina Beach, is the oldest continuously published weekly newspaper in the state of Florida. It wasn't the first newspaper on Amelia Island, though. That honor belongs to *El Telegrafo de las Floridas*.

The first thing a shrewd reader may notice about *El Telegrafo* is that its title is in Spanish, not English. That's because it resulted from Amelia's old, audacious friends, Gregor MacGregor and Louis Aury.

Scotsman MacGregor mail-ordered a printing press after capturing Amelia in 1817. He departed shortly thereafter, driven out by fear of gathering Spanish forces, and left his press behind.

Privateer Louis Aury arrived to take control of the situation. He understood the power of propaganda and diplomacy in a way that men of action rarely do. The Frenchman went so far as to recruit a lawyer and a Peruvian journalist as means to ingratiate himself into the international community.

The journalist's name was Vincent Pazos. On December 9, 1817, he used to press to print a pamphlet with the breathless title *Report of the Committee Appointed to Frame the Plan of Provisional Government for the Republic of Floridas*. Ten days later, Pazos produced the first issue of *El Telegrafo de las Floridas*. It would also be the last. Aury gave up the island thirteen days later, surrendering to Major James Bankhead and Commodore J.D. Henley on December 23, 1817.

We know a bit about what the newspaper was like because of the reaction from a *Charleston Courier* editor out of South Carolina. He read a copy sent to him by a courier. His remarks paint the picture of a blatant propaganda rag. He reported that the paper "abounds in editorial remarks upon the future destinie [*sic*] of the Republic of Florida and with sentiments of contempt and hatred for the government of Spain."

Pazos continued writing with great dramatic flair in attempted legal defenses of his former employer after Aury was booted from Amelia. Never again would he publish *El Telegrafo de las Floridas*.

Chapter 10

American Beach: Recreation and Relaxation Without Humiliation

Exterior—100 Feet in the Air—Dusk

We're looking down on the vastness of the Atlantic Ocean. A sound catches our attention, music unlike any music we've ever heard before—jazz. Our gaze turns toward the music, toward the shore, where stands a squat, white cinderblock building with a long, three-walled wooden dining structure stretching southward from it—open side facing us, exposing the jubilant tumult of dozens of people cutting up, laughing, cracking open bottles of beer. People roam in and out, cavorting in the beach's sands.

The year is 1935. The place is Evan's Rendezvous on American Beach, one of Florida's first beaches for Black Americans. It's new, unlike anything we've seen before.

Intrigued, we head toward the music…

American Beach was the brainchild of Black entrepreneur Abraham Lincoln Lewis. It was one of Florida's first beach resorts for African Americans and attracted visitors from other states, including a steady flow of busses running from Georgia and South Carolina. Lewis opened it in 1935.

From that year to 1964, the place was a magnet for human energy, with families packing the sands by day and revelers cramming into the clubs and restaurants by night. Notable celebrities ranging from Ray Charles to Joe Louis frequented the spot. It was a true destination for families, couples and singles alike and seemed to be on an unstoppable upward trajectory.

Only a good thing could slow it down—and then it did.

Vintage photograph of American Beach. *A.L. Lewis Museum at American Beach.*

Abraham Lincoln Lewis

When it comes to historical significance, "Abraham Lincoln" is a name that few people can measure up to. Abraham Lincoln Lewis, however, made an admirable attempt.

Lewis was born in 1865, the first in his family born after slavery ended. In 1876, when he was eleven, he and his family moved to Jacksonville from Madison County, Florida. He dropped out of school at thirteen and took a job in a sawmill. Despite lacking a formal education, he became Florida's first Black millionaire.

Lewis's most profitable venture was the Afro-American Life Insurance Company, which he and six other men founded on April 1, 1901. Lewis had a great talent for seeing opportunity in challenge. Black Americans had difficulty getting insurance, so Lewis started a company to fulfill the need.

Slavery had ended, but because of Jim Crow laws, Black Americans were unable to enjoy the recreational opportunities available to Whites. To change that, Lewis founded the Lincoln Golf and Country Club in Jacksonville, the first country club in the area specifically for Black Americans. Lewis also started the Negro Business League. Through it all, he built a multigenerational fortune that set his children and grandchildren up for success.

Vintage photograph of Abraham Lincoln Lewis. *A.L. Lewis Museum at American Beach.*

Yet Lewis wasn't merely driven by ambition. He spent his life giving back to Black Americans and looking for ways to improve their lives. He gave substantial sums to Edward Waters College and Bethune-Cookman College, both Black colleges. Now he wanted to create a place where his people could enjoy the surf. As he put it, they deserved a place of "recreation and relaxation without humiliation" (as documented in author Marsha Dean Phelts's *An American Beach for African Americans*).

On January 31, 1935, Lewis purchased thirty-three acres of beachfront property through the Afro-American Insurance's Pension Bureau. He opened it to the public and named it American Beach. He added 100 more acres in 1937 and 83 more in 1946, for a total of 216 acres. Parcels were sold for people to build houses.

The beach saw upward of ten thousand visitors on weekends. Tourists came from all around to walk the beach or hit the restaurants and nightclubs. It became a hot spot for Black celebrities. On any given day, a person could see legendary musicians like Ray Charles, America's great writer and folklorist Zora Neale Hurston or boxing champion Joe Louis.

American Beach was ultimately done in by good news. The Civil Rights Act of 1964 created an interesting paradox. In a 1993 piece from the *Tampa Tribune*, Marsha Dean Phelts phrased it this way: "We killed the beach through integration."

That perspective may ruffle some feathers, but few can lay better claim to having a qualified opinion on the matter. In '97, the University Press of Florida published Phelts's *An American Beach for African Americans*, which exhaustively tells the beach's story. Once the Civil Rights Act desegrated Florida's beaches, Black Americans could visit beaches closer to their homes.

As interest dried up, the area ceased to be a financially viable enterprise. Yet it wouldn't disappear completely. Largely through the efforts of the "Beach Lady," MaVynee Betsch, American Beach would be recognized as a historically significant place. Today, the American Beach Historic District consists of forty acres.

Lewis passed away on March 10, 1947, at eighty-two years old. His remains were placed in the Lewis Mausoleum in Memorial Cemetery in

Jacksonville. His wife, Mary Sammis Lewis, is there with him. Her story is interesting, as she was the great-granddaughter of Zephaniah Kingsley and Anna Madgigine Jai. Kingsley built several plantations and traded profitably in slaves. Jai, a Senegalese woman, had been a slave herself.

Lewis's impact on the world continued through his progeny. His daughter, anthropologist Johnetta B. Cole, was nominated to be the first woman president of two universities: Spelman College in Atlanta, Georgia, and Bennett College in Greensboro, North Carolina. His son, John Betsch, earned international fame as a jazz drummer.

Then, of course, there's Lewis's great-granddaughter, the Beach Lady.

The Beach Lady

"Getting the most from the least and living peacefully in harmony with nature is the most rewarding lifestyle."

—*MaVynee Betsch*

As great-granddaughter of Abraham Lincoln Lewis, MaVynee Betsch grew up in wealth and privilege. Born in 1935, she was in her physical prime during the hedonistic 1970s, when the term *jet set* was coined. It was becoming romantic for rich people flaunt their money and live like rockstars, and the era of celebrity worship was just getting started. Yet Betsch, who'd become a celebrity herself, chose a different and more soulful path.

Young Betsch was a piano prodigy. She attended the Oberlin Conservatory of Music in Ohio to build on her talents, but when she saw the opera *Aida*, she decided to switch to singing. She earned her bachelor's degree in 1955 and moved to Europe to sing professionally for a decade, mostly in German opera. The German people were intrigued by her skin tone and considered her "exotic" without any of the stigma she encountered in the United States. The Germans called her *Halbnegrin*, meaning "demi-negress."

Betsch loved her life as a singer until the success became overwhelming. She was being flooded with too much work, and opera houses were trying to lock her down in exclusive contracts for big chunks of time. Money had never been the prime motivator for a woman born into it. She headed home to Florida.

Shortly after returning home, Betsch was diagnosed with ovarian cancer. She got a hysterectomy, but the pain continued, and doctors suspected the

Vintage photograph of MaVynne "Beach Lady" Betsch. *Amelia Island Museum of History.*

cancer had spread to her colon. Betsch did something many would consider crazy today, but which was even more incredible in her time: she decided to leave the medical system behind and use natural methods to cure herself.

Betsch ate only organic foods and moved into a resort home she'd inherited. She painted the house orange and blue, knocked all the interior walls out and thought about how she actually wanted to live her life. She dug deep to override her social programming and uncover the yearning in her core.

Betsch's sign came when she saw butterflies covering an oleander bush. The image struck her as a mystical signal. With it, she began to feel well again, emotionally, psychologically and spiritually. Everything about her perspective on life transformed.

Betsch started giving her money away, mostly to environmental causes. She donated to rainforest protection groups, dune preservation efforts and butterfly studies. She gave so much money to the latter, in fact, that a butterfly textbook was dedicated to her. From 1975 onwards, she immersed herself in nature and dedicated her life to its preservation. By the 1980s, she had entire walls covered in canceled checks from her donations.

Vintage photograph of MaVynne "Beach Lady" Betsch. *Amelia Island Museum of History.*

To protect sea turtle eggs, Betsch had signs posted around the beach marking their nests. She pushed residents to plant flowers as a way to provide a habitat for butterflies. She planted trees along Lewis Street and led historical tours to keep the memory of American Beach alive. She'd jettisoned her life of pomp and privilege—and she loved it. Speaking to Russ Rymer for a 2003 Smithsonian interview, she said, "It's a state of mind. I think everyone should have a life-threatening something-or-other. Because then you don't take it all for granted anymore."

Betsch moved into rooms owned by Afro-American Insurance, but she was forced out after her cousin, James L. Lewis, lost control of the company. In 1985, a new president was brought in. He ordered Betsch to leave the property. She headed back to the beach.

The fifty-year-old woman wandered the sands for some time, moving through the night to avoid being attacked in her sleep, resting on the porches of houses without owners. Fortunately, some people remembered Betsch and started helping her out. The owners of her great-grandfather's first American Beach home allowed her to sleep on the sands in front of the house. People gave her food and offered opportunities to housesit.

Betsch's look increasingly evolved into an attention-grabber. She became a political billboard with dozens of buttons balanced out by seashells. A tall woman at six feet, she grew an additional six feet of dreadlocks that she bundled into a hairnet and carried around her waist.

Betsch's sister Johnetta Cole sent her money every month. Cole was (and still is) a prominent educator and anthropologist. In addition to cash, she gave Betsch a motor home. Betsch transformed that motor home into a museum with books on all ranges of subjects. She'd leave the door unlocked so that anyone could come study for free.

Betsch did a lot for Amelia Island's natural habitat, but her most significant contribution might be saving American Beach. She protected it from the development of luxury condominiums and gave free tours to visitors, keeping Abraham Lincoln Lewis's remarkable story alive.

Betsch passed away from cancer on September 5, 2005. The Dalai Lama recognized her as an Unsung Hero of Compassion. She remains one of Amelia's most beloved figures.

Before Betsch passed, she tasked friends with missions to protect American Beach. One of them, Pastor Carlton Jones, told *First Coast News*, "It all goes back to the Beach Lady. She inspired and, before she passed, she talked to about three people, Carol Owens Alexander, myself, and I can't remember the other person, and she basically gave each of us a task, is to protect the beach. And so that is part of what we do."

NaNa Dune

One of Betsch's notable successes was securing the preservation of NaNa, Florida's tallest sand dune at sixty feet. It's on historic American Beach, just off Ocean Boulevard, where the road meets Lewis Street. Betsch gave the dune its "NaNa" name and was the driving force in having it designated as a protected landmark. It's an important habitat for the gopher tortoise and the painted bunting.

NaNa is really a dune system rather than a singular dune. Part of that system is called Little NaNa Dune. Little NaNa almost lost its protected status in 2021, but conservation groups inspired by Betsch's legacy leapt to its defense. They worked with the North Florida Land Trust to win a loan of over $1 million to protect Little NaNa.

The president of the North Florida Land Trust, Jim McCarthy, told *First Coast News*, "We wanted to protect this historic community and its natural benefits for the good of the wildlife that depends on it, and to protect the sense of place that rests in the memories of so many generations of families that vacationed in American Beach at a time when they were prohibited from beaches all across this country."

Evans's Rendezvous

> *"From 1948 until 1980, a visitor might come to American Beach and never go in the water, but it seemed impossible that a visitor could come to American Beach and fail to go into Evans's Rendezvous."*
> —*Marsha Dean Phelts,* An American Beach for African Americans

Remember that white cinderblock building we saw on our introduction to American Beach? That building was Evans's Rendezvous. For roughly forty years, it was the hottest spot on American Beach, if not the entire eastern Florida coastline.

Willie Brantley Evans was born on August 5, 1915, in Orangeburg, South Carolina. He went to American Beach in 1940 while working as a cook in the Civilian Conservation Corps, part of President Franklin Delano Roosevelt's New Deal, which was an attempt to end the Great Depression. Evans was already showing what he was made of by running a shoeshine business in his off hours—from the start, he was driven to get ahead.

Evans took an immediate liking to American Beach and returned in 1941. He purchased a twenty-five-by-fifty-foot plot near the home of Abraham

Vintage photograph of Evans's Rendezvous. *Amelia Island Museum of History.*

Lincoln Lewis. His friend Tom Blowers had a father who was a carpenter. Blowers's dad helped build Evans's first establishment, a yellow-painted building named Sunny's Spot. Things were looking good, but then Evans got drafted into World War II.

Evans served for four years, during which Sunny's Spot sat boarded up and ignored. When he came back to Fernandina, the entire nation was in a celebratory mood. Sunny's Spot hopped around the clock, which was great for Evans but not so great for his neighbor Lewis, who never drank, smoked or gambled. Lewis offered Evans a different property in exchange for the one that Sunny's sat on. Evans agreed.

The new Sunny's Spot became increasingly popular. To meet demand, Evans built a two-story restaurant/nightclub named Evans's Rendezvous. The new place could fit up to two hundred people. Stories suggest that it often exceeded that legal capacity. It became a bona fide destination for Black musicians and celebrities of all kinds.

On weekends, the establishment routinely filled to the point where people were crammed in like jarred pickles, shoulder to shoulder, butt to butt. Evans's place was a recreational haven for Black Americans from all around the South. We can only imagine what the excitatory energy of the place must have been like.

Evans's was a wild, rowdy drinker's haven at night, but it was just as busy during the day as families bussed in from South Carolina and Georgia to enjoy the restaurant. Evans's Rendezvous hopped for over thirty years.

Like the rest of American Beach, Evans's Rendezvous was done in by the Civil Rights Act of 1964. Once Black Americans could recreate wherever they chose, they no longer had reason to travel all the way to American Beach. Business dried up. The high, wild energy faded away.

In 1980, Evans sold his place to retired high school football coach William Weathersbee, who renamed it Ocean Rendezvous. That restaurant closed in 2000. For years, local history buffs tried to get the Rendezvous placed under some kind of historical protection. They finally achieved their goal in 2023, when the Florida Department of State's African-American Cultural and Historical Grant awarded $500,000 to Nassau County to renovate the old hideaway.

Willie Evans passed away on August 9, 1996, four days after his eighty-first birthday.

The Evans's Rendezvous building, soon to be renovated as of this writing, stands at 5508 Gregg Street, easily visible from the road.

The Streets of American Beach

If you look at a map of historic American Beach, you'll see Lewis Street running west to east with shorter streets branching off in a northerly direction. There's a person, and a story, behind all of them.

The first four streets were named for men significant to the Afro-American Life Insurance Company (hereinafter Afro Insurance).

Lewis Street: American Beach's main road, Lewis Street was named after Abraham Lincoln Lewis. It leads to the beach.

Gregg Street: The first north–south street from the beach, Gregg Street was named after Reverend Elias J. Gregg. He was a pastor and the first president of Afro Insurance (when it was still called Afro-American Industrial and Benefit Association).

Waldron Street: Just west of Gregg is Waldron, which was named after J. Milton Waldron, also a pastor. He was the first to conceive of Afro Insurance.

Price Street: Price Street doesn't run all the way to Lewis, but a portion still exists one block up. It bears the name of Reverend Alfred W. Price. He was the third Afro Insurance president and builder of many successful entrepreneurial ventures. His grandson married Zora Neale Hurston.

After the first four, the streets tell still other stories.

Ervin Street: Named for Louis Dargon Ervin, a self-made man that some sources cite as Afro Insurance's first sales agent (others say he was "one of" the first). He rose through the ranks to vice president. His vacation home in Fernandina was dubbed Ervin's Rest, which was added to the National Register of Historic Places in 1998. It's memorialized by a historical marker at the intersection of Julia and Gregg Streets. The house still stands and is the only oceanfront house in American Beach that still has its original structure.

Julia Street: Julia is named for Julia Brown Lewis, Abraham's mother. It runs parallel to Lewis Street and is oriented east–west.

Mary Street: Named for Abraham's first wife, Mary Lewis.

Burney Road: The last street built on American Beach, Burney Road is named for I.H. Burney II, Afro Insurance president from 1967 to 1975.

Franklintown

Before American Beach, there was Franklintown. Unlike the former, which is enjoying renewed interest, the latter is nearly forgotten. If not for the efforts of Marsha Dean Phelts, who pieced the story together from oral histories of descendants of the Franklintown inhabitants, it might have fallen off the radar completely.

Major General William T. Sherman issued Special Field Order No. 15 on January 16, 1865, about four months before the official end of the Civil War. The order dictated that a swath of islands and mainland—largely that of the old plantations, from Charleston, South Carolina, to the St. Johns River in Florida—would be designated as land for freed slaves to live on. Some of Amelia's Black residents decided to move to Franklintown, with the first families likely coming predominantly from the freed slaves from the Harrison Plantation.

Franklin himself never owned anything of Franklintown. No one is exactly sure why his name was even given to the place. In 1872, he offered to purchase some property from a man named Albert Cone. Cone agreed, but the deal never materialized. How exactly that led to the area being named Franklintown, no one is sure.

The original Franklintown families lived off the land, whether through hunting and fishing, animal husbandry or farming. Nature was bountiful then, and people could cast seine nets from the shore into the water and watch them fill, almost instantly, with fish.

Franklintown still exists as an unincorporated community on southern Amelia Island, but much of the original land was sold to the Amelia Island Company, which today is Omni Amelia Island Resort. It still holds its original Franklintown Cemetery, which descendants have protected from development to this day.

Franklintown United Methodist Church

The Franklintown Chapel was a center of social life. Before the chapel, there was an open-air congregation that started in 1880, with Reverend J.G. Howard serving as its first pastor from 1880 to 1885. Gabriel Means, an ex-slave who'd joined the Union army and fought in the Civil War, and his wife, Edith, donated land for a church in 1888. In 1892, Gabriel built the original Franklin Chapel.

That church stood until 1949, when the building was ruined as part of the State Road A1A construction project. A new chapel was built to replace it. When the Amelia Island Company bought up Franklintown in 1972, the chapel was moved to American Beach. It still stands at Franklintown United Methodist Church at 2012 1415 Lewis Street, American Beach. Just off the road is a historical marker discussing the chapel.

Chapter 11
Amelia Forts

Fort San Carlos

Fernandina Plaza Historic State Park sits atop a bluff at the northern end of Amelia. It's managed by Fort Clinch State Park but preserves a different structure: Fort San Carlos. Or perhaps we should say it preserves about one-third of that historical site. Archaeologists estimate that two-thirds has eroded away.

Spain built Fort San Carlos in 1816, three years after jettisoning George Mathews and his Patriots. It was built of earthworks and wood in the shape of a lunette fortification, which is basically a half-moon shape (the defenders of the Alamo used a lunette fortification). The fort could hold up to ten pieces of artillery. Its primary purpose was to defend the Amelia River harbor.

Fort San Carlos saw much of Amelia's military action. On June 29, 1817, it was the installation surrendered to Gregor MacGregor and his imaginary one-thousand-man army. When MacGregor abandoned the island, he left a handful of men (estimates have been as high as twenty-five) behind with Jared Irwin. The fort helped the small group repel a much larger Spanish force during the Battle of Amelia Island. An army of three hundred men and two gunboats was forced to flee.

Shortly after, Irwin allowed French Corsair Louis Aury inside. Irwin was willing to take a chance because he needed funds and reinforcements. So Fort San Carlos technically stood undefeated, as Irwin had simply chosen not to use it.

During the Civil War, the Confederate army occupied Fort San Carlos, but the installation wasn't involved in any battles. U.S. forces used it during the Spanish-American War of 1898, but again, it saw no significant action.

Fort Clinch

Spain started fortifying the area of Fort Clinch in 1736. At that point, it was all earthworks and simple wooden construction. Construction on the fort proper started with the U.S. Army Corps of Engineers in 1847. They had completed about two-thirds of it when the Civil War broke out.

Aerial photograph of Fort Clinch. *Amelia Island Museum of History.*

The Confederates took control of the fort during their brief possession of Amelia in 1862. In March that year, the Union took the island back and resumed building. They never did complete the fort, but the U.S. army maintained control up to 1898. With the start of the Spanish-American war, the army stored munitions and housed soldiers in Fort Clinch. The Americans added weapons and additional fortifications, but they never went into use.

In 1926, having sat unused for decades, Clinch was sold to private interests. In 1935, it became one of the first state parks in Florida. It's remained a tourist destination ever since, other than a brief period during World War II when it was used as a communications center.

Chapter 12

Plantations

Harrison Plantation and Harrison Family Cemetery

The Harrison Plantation once stood beside Harrison Creek. The countryside and Omni Amelia Island Resort have long since swallowed up the remnants of the location. Only the Harrison Family Cemetery, which contains a historical plaque discussing the Harrison family, still exists today.

Samuel and Isabel McQueen English Harrison started the plantation in 1792 after moving from Yorktown, Virginia, on September 30, 1791. They brought with them three sons and seven slaves, the latter of which wound up being the plantation's most lasting contribution to Amelia.

The Harrisons homesteaded on land offered to them by Governor Juan Nepomuceno de Quesada y Barnuevo Arrocha, with an agreement that they'd farm it productively for ten years and then receive full legal rights to the property. The new plantation included the site where Chief Micoa and Father Francesco Simon de Sales had resettled the Gaule tribe back in 1686.

In 1862, during the Civil War, Union forces destroyed the Harrison Plantation. It's believed that, after Major General Sherman issued Special Field Order No. 15, which liberated former plantation lands for use by freed slaves, it was the old Harrison Plantation slaves who started Franklintown (hence the previous comment about them being the plantation's most lasting contribution).

In 1972, Amelia Island Plantation, today named Omni Amelia Island Resort, purchased the land the Harrison Plantation once stood on. All that remains of the original plantation is the Harrison Family Cemetery, which includes several Harrison family members. Neither Samuel nor Isabel has a headstone there, but it's possible they were buried with wooden markers that have since disintegrated. In modern times, Native American remains were interred in the Harrison Cemetery following their discovery during an archaeological dig in the area.

Yellow Bluff Plantation and the Fernandez Preserve

The Fernandez Preserve is all that remains of Yellow Bluff Plantation. It's relatively small, but it's beautiful and open to public viewing.

Domingo and Maria Fernández (Maria was born Maria Mattair, daughter of famed Mary Mattair) started Yellow Plantation in 1793. Domingo was a gunboat captain and received his land through the last Spanish land grant ever given in Florida (it was also Florida's largest land grant plantation). The couple raised beef and dairy cows while growing vegetables and oranges. After Maria passed, she willed the plantation to her sons. In 1853, they sold it to agents of Senator David Yulee, one of whom was our old friend Joseph Finegan, whose house was turned into an orphanage by Chloe Merrick.

The family burial plot was left behind. Today's it's called the Fernandez Preserve or Villalonga Park, presumably after Leonilla Villalonga, the last person buried there. She passed in 1915 and granted $15,000 to be kept for permanent maintenance of the site. The location is outside St. Michael's Parish Church.

Chapter 13

Amelia Changes the Modern Shrimping Industry

People have been eating shrimp since long before the written word existed. No place we know of can lay claim to inventing shrimping. Credit goes to whoever was the first prehistoric person to look at the odd little animal and think, "I wonder what that tastes like?"

Fernandina Beach, however, did birth some significant advancements in the shrimping industry, so much so that in 2015, Gray Edenfield's book *Amelia Island: Birthplace of the Modern Shrimping Industry* was published. In the following sections, we'll explore some of those advances.

T.E. Fischer

T.E. Fischer was king of Amelia Island shrimpers in the 1880s. His story is informative for understanding how the industry worked back in the day, because the big issue with shrimp, beyond how to catch them, is how to store them. In Fischer's day, preservation was done by boiling shrimp in brine, laying them out on a wooden platform and letting them dry in the sun.

Remarkably, that simple technique was effective enough to allow Fischer to transport enough shrimp to create a veritable empire. He had outlets running from Savannah, Georgia, to New York. At his peak in 1879, he put out twenty-nine thousand pounds of shrimp. The very next year, he shut down the enterprise, citing "bad returns from dealers."

Two shrimp boats head out for shrimping. *Amelia Island Museum of History. State Library and Archives of Florida.*

A NEW WAY TO SHRIMP

Two stories surround the arrival of Sicilian Solicito "Mike" Salvador on Amelia Island. The most common is that the hurricane of 1898 forced his ship to dock in Fernandina. The other is that he moved to the United States in 1895, traveling to New Orleans on a banana boat (as in a boat literally delivering bananas). He rode a train up through Cedar Key in western Florida and over to Fernandina, where he took note of the fisheries and decided to move.

Whichever is true, Salvador changed the shrimping business forever.

Salvador went by the name Mike because it was easier for most in the United States to pronounce. He made his money by fishing and acting as an interpreter. With his income, he bought a boat and all the equipment

Burbank nets drying in the sun after being dipped in poly sealant. *State Library and Archives of Florida.*

he needed to start his own shrimping business. What did it take to launch a business in 1899? Well, we happen to know precisely:

- 150 pounds of powder for preservation
- Boat
- Casting net
- Ten-gallon boiler
- Twenty kegs
- Two ice boxes (one small, one large)

With the items from that simple list, Salvador created an empire.

Salvador made advances in a few areas, working with his brother-in-law Salvatore Versaggi and friend Anthony Poli. Before that, though, a major development contributed to the viability of the shrimping industry: the 1895 invention of refrigerated box cars. From that point forward, shrimp could be transported long distances without going bad.

As for the Salvador trio, they started using motorized boats in 1902, significantly widening the range in which they could shrimp, as well as increasing the size of their hauls. They also adopted a modified otter trawl

Al Saperstein from WUFT-TV preparing to shoot the Burbank net shop, Fernandina Beach, Florida. *State Library and Archives of Florida.*

net, which supposedly increased catch sizes by a factor of ten. Perhaps their most significant advancement, though, was in logistics.

As a team, the three Sicilians blew the shrimp market wide open. They established processing and distribution points in Savannah, Atlanta, Philadelphia, New York City and Boston. Eventually, they supplied Canada and Denmark. They created a whole new market for the food.

Shrimp had always been an expensive delicacy, so most people didn't even think to shop for it. Salvador and team convinced big city restauranteurs to give shrimp out for free so that people could develop a taste for it, opening up brand new middle- and lower-class markets.

The men created a shrimping empire that was the core piece of the Fernandina economy in the early and middle 1900s. Hundreds of boats filled the waters around Amelia. They weren't just American. Shrimpers came from Portugal, Scandinavia and Salvador's native Sicily. With this boon, other businesses popped up to supply the shrimpers. Ultimately, Amelia's Salvador-born shrimping boom was done in by its own success. As word spread, the shrimpers harvested their product faster than it could replenish itself.

Salvador passed away in 1921 at fifty-five years old. Versaggi followed in 1925 and Poli in 1945.

Amelia's Master Boatbuilder

Michael Nichlos Tiliakos moved to the United States from Greece at just eighteen years old. He settled in Tarpon Springs in western Florida before moving to Fernandina in 1912 for an Irish girl named Clara Franks. Tiliakos must have been a remarkably patient man because he stuck around until 1912, when Clara finally married him. That patience paid off, not only in terms of marital bliss but also because he built a business that lasted for fifty years.

One of Tiliakos's best builders was Dematrios Nicholas Deonas, who left school at nine to learn boatbuilding. He was born in 1909 on Santorini, a Greek island. He was known as Jimmy and wound up in Fernandina in 1941. He created the Super Trawler, an enormous shrimping boat that employed double-rigged nets. His design changed the entire industry and soon became the norm in the business.

Deonas opened his own business with Taliakos's blessing. They were collaborators rather than competitors. Taliakos arranged the marriage between Deonas and his daughter Anna. People from all around the country ordered ships from the two men.

Amelia's Master Net Makers

In 1915, Bill Burbank Sr. (Cap'n Bill to locals) owned a shrimping boat. One day, he started making his own nets, using the smaller holes he'd seen used for North Carolina bluefish. He added a wing to his trawler to make the net taller, increasing its holding capacity. He was doing the work for his own fishing and had no idea it would lead to building a business that would stand for over one hundred years.

Fellow shrimpers and fishermen noticed how good Burbank's nets were. Soon, he was making nets more than he was fishing. In 1957, he passed the business on to his son, Bill Burbank Jr., who named it Burbank Trawl Makers Inc. Burbank Sr. passed away in 1975. In the '90s, the business went to Jr.'s son, also named Bill.

Changes in fuel prices and government regulations inspired Burbank III to make sports nets to supplement his business's income, and the company made its first batting cage in 1979.

The company started making sports nets with ultra-high-molecular-weight polyethylene fiber that had originally been designed to help shrimpers save money on fuel. Starting with the Chicago White Sox, this innovation became the norm in professional baseball. The shop still stands; its operations are now on the former site of Fernandina's old Pogy Plant.

Chapter 14

About Town

Bosque Bello: The Beautiful Forest Where Fernandina's Dead Speak

At 1321 North Fourteenth Street, close to the entrance to Old Town Fernandina, the Bosque Bello cemetery crouches like a meditating toad among ancient cedars. Its tombstones tell the tales of Amelia Islanders going all the way back to 1813—and possibly earlier. Some researchers suspect that Native American tribes used it for the same purpose long before Europeans arrived.

The Spanish name Bosque Bello means "beautiful forest." It was established in 1798 on land granted to the city by plantation owner Domingo Fernandez. The city added more cemetery coverage in the 1940s with property donated by J.G. and Sadie Cooper. Today, Bosque Bello occupies roughly twenty-nine acres of land.

The oldest grave in the cemetery belongs to a French soldier named Peter Bouisou de Nicar, laid to rest on January 9, 1813. Little else is known of him other than that he was a fifty-six-year-old Freemason and a native of Cape Francois and he had children named Jacques and Rosina. He was a captain in the French Gens d'Arme—a rather auspicious title.

Both Confederate and Union soldiers are buried in Bosque Bello. There are headstones marked in English, Portuguese, German, French and Spanish. Because the cemetery has been falling into disrepair over recent decades, advocates have been organizing restoration plans since 2018. The site's historical importance is widely understood, as is its appeal as a recreation area—it was named "beautiful forest" for a reason, and it remains a location to admire for its picturesque natural beauty as well as its place in island history.

For explorers: Bosque Bello is located less than half a mile north of McClure's Hill.

Old Town Fernandina, Where the Streets Have Moved

Old Town Fernandina is the name used for the town's original location. It's still part of Fernandina Beach, of course, but it's no longer the central downtown area. This is a historical anomaly, really, when one considers the fact that Timucuan Indians were living there for thousands of years before Europeans even knew it existed.

Old Town was platted by Spain in 1811, making it the last city in the Western Hemisphere built according to Spanish colonial platting rules (Spain had an extensive series of requirements, a kind of instruction manual, that all its colonies were legally required to follow). Old Town was added to the U.S. National Register of Historic Places on January 29, 1990. The area once contained Fort San Carlos, which is no longer in existence but played an important role in the island's early post-European-contact history (the fort appears multiple times in this book). The spot is memorialized as Plaza San Carlos and can be visited today.

The city was moved in order to be near the Florida Railroad completed in 1861 by Senator David Levy Yulee. The railroad's terminus point was in Fernandina. Its completion was a major event in state history as it was the first time that east and west Florida were joined by train transit. The railroad was expected to bring in a whole new world of commerce, so the entire town was moved up around it.

Probably the First Inn on Fernandina Beach

George Clarke's zoning records leave many interesting tidbits of information. For instance, we know that in March 1809, Half Lot 11 was granted to

Francisco de Salas, born in Torre Guemada, Old Castillo, Spain. Salas petitioned Governor Enrique White, explaining that he'd spent most of his life at sea and built up enough fortune to buy some land.

Salas asked White for permission to build an inn capable of fitting twenty to thirty people. White inquired to Military Commandant Justo López, who agreed that the town could use an inn. "The petition was granted," the zoning records state, "and Salas built his inn—probably the first at Fernandina."

GOLDEN AGE OF AMELIA ISLAND (1869–1915)

The hurricane of 1898 must have blown in some kind of magic, because Amelia Island entered its golden age in the aftermath.

Things like "golden ages" are rarely neatly defined or easy to quantify, but Amelia's boom time is generally considered to have stretched from the

Vintage photograph of burning phosphate elevator. August 19, 1907. *Amelia Island Museum of History.*

late 1800s into the early 1900s. This was a time when Fernandina produced huge amounts of shrimp. The success of that industry radiated outward, rippling throughout the island.

Fernandina further developed a wildly successful naval stores industry—naval stores being conifer products like pine oil, rosin, tall oil and turpentine. The term comes from the fact that those products are used in the construction of wooden ships. From 1905 to 1923, Fernandina had the most profitable naval stores industry in the entire country.

The lumber industry also took off, but it was phosphate that truly elevated Amelia. U.S. marshal, journalist and engineer Albertus Vogt discovered the substance in central Florida. He picked up the scent when he looked into a spring and saw fossils that reminded him of fossils he'd seen in South Carolina, where he knew phosphate to be located. His find kicked off a phosphate rush of sorts, with Amelia perfectly positioned to export the stuff. One of the phosphate plants was named the Florida Terminal Company, and it exported more than four hundred thousand tons of the materials to Europe.

Most of Amelia's grand homes and buildings came from the golden age period. You can feel the presence of the era as you walk the streets. The spirit of the boom time has been woven into the city. It's a big part of the city's spirit, the energy that draws tourists there today.

HARD TIMES, COUNTY SEAT FERNANDINA

Fernandina Beach is the county seat for Nassau County. As far as can be pieced together from records, it has held that position since 1824, when the county was founded, except for one stretch from 1835 to 1840. In the story of that excluded period, one can get an idea of what Amelia looked like at the time.

Fernandina lost its place as the county seat because so few people were doing business in town. Moving such governmental operations is rarely easy or cheap, and it must have been doubly difficult in a time when transportation was limited and roads were rough. So we can assume the situation was pretty bleak to inspire such a decision.

From 1835 to 1840, the seat moved to a mysterious place named Court House Ditch. Very little is known of Ditch other than that it sat between Fernandina and King's Ferry, about twenty miles west of Fernandina. Court

House Ditch is the most used name for this place, but records also have it as "Court House" and "Nassau."

In 1840, the seat swung back to Fernandina as things turned around for the town. In 1842, Fernandina was designated as protected land due to the military importance of its harbor, and the Council of the Territory of Florida incorporated the city on an eight-year deal.

Then, in 1853, news went out that a cross-state railroad would terminate in Fernandina. The news made the town considerably more attractive. Real estate spiked in value, the population grew to 1,390 people and more ships appeared in port. Pirates and raiders hung about, making things difficult for everybody, but the situation turned around, taking a decidedly more upward trajectory.

Cotton and timber became major exports. Shops sprang up to outfit the commercial ships, creating a whole industry that would be a staple of Fernandina for years. Fernandina was well on its way to becoming the jewel of the South by 1861.

Then the Civil War came along and threw everything off the rails.

The Yellow Fever of 1877

Yellow fever earned its name from the fact that it causes liver damage that gives people yellow-tinted skin. It's primarily spread through bites from the *Aedes aegypt* mosquito. The disease spreads fast and is prone to causing epidemics. Amelia suffered more than one such outbreak, but 1877 was possibly the worst of them (1888 hit hard, as well).

It's believed that this particular outbreak in 1877 resulted from sailors who came in from the West Indies, but no one is sure. What we know is that in August 1877, the fever started to spread. It flew under the radar for a bit, but when a family of four died in September, it was clear that the ailment wasn't a common cold.

Many residents fled Amelia. Those who stuck around had to deal with 1,100 sick people, which led to all commerce on the island falling more and more behind. This was the outbreak during which the brave Sisters of St. Joseph cared for the sick. By the time it was over, the outbreak had claimed 94 lives, including those of Sister Marie de Sales Kennedy and Mother Marie Celenie Joubert.

FLORIDA HOUSE INN

Somewhere between 1857 and 1859, David Yulee had the Florida Inn built to act as a boardinghouse. He was trying to complete a railroad that would connect Fernandina Beach to Cedar Key in Levy County on the western Florida coast and wanted a place to house investors, executives and influential people interested in the project. It was long assumed that the railroad itself built the inn, but Rob Hull with the Amelia Island Museum of History turned up research indicating it was actually a man named Peter Gill Peterson.

Whatever the case, Yulee did eventually complete his railroad (see the section "The Train That Exploded"), and the Florida House Inn has remained in almost continuous operation since its opening.

With the start of the Civil War, the inn was used to house Union soldiers. Over the years, it passed through many hands. Its earliest records are somewhat bewildering, but we get into the meat of things with the Leddies.

On January 28, 1873, the property deed was signed over to Annie Leddy, wife of Union major Leddy. Major Leddy was thirty-nine or forty years old. He'd moved to northern Florida after being named provost marshal of the region. He passed away in October, eight months after buying the inn, from "complications from battle wounds in breast and left arm," leading one to guess that he deeded the house to his wife because he knew his time was short.

Annie ran the building as a combined hotel and boardinghouse. She added to the building and connected the kitchen and main house. When another boardinghouse popped up next door, Annie absorbed it into her own establishment (after helping the newcomers out for nine years).

Annie operated the inn through some of Fernandina's golden age. She passed away in 1908. By 1990, the building was on the verge of being condemned. The Warners stepped in and remodeled it. It's gone through multiple owners since but has consistently kept its doors open.

Guests of the Florida Inn have included automotive giant Henry Ford, comedy duo Laurel and Hardy, actress Mary Pickford, eighteenth president of the United States Ulysses S. Grant, Cuban poet José Martí, and Lucy Carnegie, heiress to the famously wealthy Carnegie family.

Today, the hotel is rumored to house multiple ghosts. The paranormal, sadly, is out of bounds for this text, but the author recommends *Ghosts of Amelia & Other Tales* by Maggie Carter-de Vries for those with spooky interests.

Amelia Island Light

Smack dab in the middle of Amelia Island's north end, not far from Egan's Creek, Florida's oldest functioning lighthouse stands atop a sixty-foot-high bluff. It's there to warn ships approaching from the Atlantic, St. Mary's River and Cumberland Sound. The lighthouse lays claim to multiple interesting qualities. For one, it's the westernmost lighthouse on the East Coast of the United States, due to its being located three-quarters of a mile inland.

The lighthouse was built in 1838 from the deconstructed materials of another lighthouse that had been built eighteen years earlier on Cumberland Island, Georgia. That original structure was moved after changes to the channel hampered the beacon's effectiveness. Amelia Island Light stands sixty-four feet high. It was originally fifty, but a lantern added in 1881 brought it to sixty-four. It cast its first duty light in 1839.

In its original build, the lighthouse had fourteen lamps, each with fourteen-inch reflectors. They were increased to fifteen inches in 1848. It was fully electrified in 1933 and, by 1970, fully automated.

The Coast Guard owned and operated the lighthouse for much of its history but gave it to the City of Fernandina Beach on March 28, 2001, after

Vintage photograph of the Amelia Island Light. *Amelia Island Museum of History.*

it was declared to be an unneeded "surplus" item by the National Historic Lighthouse Preservation Act. In 2002, the Florida Division of Historical Resources granted the city $350,000 for restoration of the lighthouse. The light still serves its original purpose, but the tower is maintained as a historical site only. The city maintains the monument, while the Coast Guard handles the beacon itself.

The lighthouse's distance from shore has contributed to its longevity. More sheltered from the elements than most lighthouses, it has been in a good state of repair while most other similar structures its age have long since fallen apart. Up to sixteen other lighthouses were built in the United States from 1821 to 1845, and none of them withstood the test of time.

Some points interest about the Amelia Island Light:

- Winslow Lewis designed it, as he did many American lighthouses built in the early 1800s. He returned to oversee the reconstruction that took place after the lighthouse was moved from Cumberland Island.
- The lighthouse has a hand-cut granite spiral stairway inside.
- The tower is made of brick encased by a metal cupola.
- The beacon flashes every ten seconds, a signature practice that acts as a marker of the lighthouse's identity. The flash is visible sixteen nautical miles away.
- It was operated by a total of twenty-one lightkeepers from 1838 to 1954, at which point it was automated.
- Formerly, the tower was accompanied by three houses that functioned as residences for the lightkeepers. None remain today.

There's a definite romance to the idea of being a lightkeeper, but the work could be rather grueling. Lightkeepers had to wind the beacon's clockworks and trim its wicks every four hours. They also had to hand-carry buckets of oil all the way up to the lantern on top, with zero opportunity for a night off. The lighthouse's position wasn't popular with some sailors that relied on it. They complained it was too far from the water. Still, once set in its place, it wasn't moved again. The lighthouse was unharmed during a brief occupation by the Confederate army and was promptly back in action once the Civil War ended.

FOR EXPLORERS: The city does two public tours every month. Contact the Atlantic Recreation Center for details. They bus you to the spot.

Centre Street Post Office

But how historic is Amelia Island, really? Well, historic enough that even its post office earns a place in the books.

Fernandina's Centre Street Post Office, also known as the United States Post Office, Custom House and Courthouse, stands on the corner of Centre and Fourth Street. It was built in 1911 or 1912. John Knox, the U.S. Treasury Department's supervising architect, designed it in the Renaissance Revival style. In addition to housing the postal service, it also operated as the customhouse overseeing seaborne commerce, both imports and exports.

The United States District Court for the Southern District of Florida met at the building for centuries. Court staff didn't stop until 1962, with the establishment of the Middle District of Florida, at which point they started using the building for that purpose.

Vintage photograph of Fernandina's Centre Street Post Office. *Amelia Island Museum of History.*

In 2019, the city attempted to purchase the building, which was valued at $2.5 million. The situation was complicated and received a fair amount of news coverage, but ultimately, the federal government decided against the sale.

The Centre Street Post Office is three stories high and encompasses 18,800 square feet. The University of Florida Press's *A Guide to Florida's Historic Architecture* includes this building in its list of notable Florida buildings.

For explorers: Half a block up Centre Street stands the Old Nassau County Courthouse and the Lesesne House.

Old Nassau County Courthouse

At 416 Centre Street, a block away from the historic Centre Street Post Office, stands the Old Nassau County Courthouse. It was built in 1891 in the Classical Revival style. Its most prominent features are the street-front bell tower and steeple. It possesses impressive Corinthian columns (one of the primary features laypeople associate with Greek architecture) and a bell designed by Meneely and Co. out of West Troy, New York.

The building was renovated in 2002 by the Auchter Company, which itself is historically notable in that it was started up in 1929. It was one of Florida's first general contractors.

A Guide to Florida's Historic Architecture, published in 1989 by the University of Florida Press, deemed the Old Nassau County Courthouse significant enough for inclusion.

For explorers: Directly across the street from the courthouse stands the Lesesne House. One block west, on Fourth, is the historic Centre Street Post Office.

Lesesne House

Standing at 415 Centre Street (about four blocks east of the Amelia Island Welcome Center) stands the Lesesne House. It may be Fernandina's oldest house still occupied as a residence.

Originally, the estate included a large olive grove. The land was sold to an unnamed entrepreneur who planned on building a hotel on the grove's land. That project never developed, and it instead became the grounds on which the historic Centre Street Post Office was built.

Vintage photograph of the Lesesne House. *Amelia Island Museum of History.*

Vintage photograph of the Lesesne House. *Amelia Island Museum of History.*

Doctor John F. Lesesne had the house built in 1860. It covered three lots (13–15) of Block 23. Lesesne also purchased lots 11 and 12, with the whole package costing him $1,000. He died during the Civil War.

His thirteen-year-old daughter, Josephine, inherited the house. In 1868, her estate sold the house to John Friend, district tax commissioner, for $3,000. Friend was born in Germany and moved to the United States in 1846 at the age of twenty-two. By 1855, he'd set up a legal practice in Ohio. He moved to Fernandina in 1865 and died in 1878 while holding the position of Nassau County state senator-elect.

The Lesesne House is a double-gallery home, which means it has two big porches, one atop the other, out front— a style commonly associated with New Orleans. The house's boxed columns are cut from singular pieces of timber. It has three chimneys. Post and beam with mortise and tenon joinery was used rather than nails.

The house had undergone many renovations over the years, each of them noted in a 1974 document created by Charles Edwin Chase for the Historic American Buildings Survey. The National Register of Historic Places added the Lesesne House to its list of properties in 1973.

For explorers: The Lesesne House is directly across the street from the Historic Court House building. One block over, on Fourth, is the Centre Street Post Office.

Captain Bell's Pippi Longstocking House

For years it was common to see German girls in pigtails bopping excitedly through Fernandina Beach and having photographs snapped before a big yellow house on 212 Estrada Street. The location had been known as the Bell House for quite some time in town, but with the release of the 1988 film *The New Adventures of Pippi Longstocking*, it unofficially became the Pippi Longstocking House.

A harbor pilot named Captain Bill Bell built the house in 1888 or 1889. It features a couple notable architectural details. The porch is a good representation of the Chinese Chippendale style that was popular in the United States in the eighteenth and nineteenth centuries. It's also an example of the Gingerbread Age, during which people loved lavishly detailed homes resembling gingerbread houses.

The 1988 Pippi Longstocking movie was filmed in Fernandina Beach, with the Bell House featured as Pippi's home, Villa Villekulla. The Longstocking character has been around since Swedish author Astrid Lidgren first penned her into life in the 1940s. The character was first rendered on film in 1969 and has appeared that way several times since. Longstocking was a staple of German culture for decades.

Robert Sands Schuyler, Architect

One man designed at least four of Fernandina's signature historic houses, as well as other buildings.

Robert Sands Schuyler made his name in New York City. He fought in the Union cavalry in the Civil War, then moved to Florida in 1881 and took the position of city clerk. He built his reputation designing churches in the Carpenter Gothic style and crafted most of Fernandina's great historical houses, including the Williams House, the Fairbanks House and the Tabby House.

While Schuyler's name isn't found much in the city, his influence is highly visible (literally).

Tabby House

The Tabby House isn't made out of tabby, but the building material is close enough to keep the name. The house was built in 1885, the same year as the Fairbanks House. It's made of bricks formed from local shells and concrete, not the lime, sand, water and oyster shell mixture that is officially "tabby" material. This house is the only one to make use of the material in the city.

C.W. Lewis, U.S. land commissioner, built the house to Schuyler's design. It's a great example of Victorian architecture, with unique features including rounded arches and elaborate balustrades.

You can visit the house at 27 South Seventh Street on the corner of Ash Street. The National Register of Historic Places includes the house.

Fairbanks House

The Fairbanks House stands at 227 South Seventh Street. Built by Major George Rainsford Fairbanks in 1885 to Schuyler's design, the house is sometimes called Fairbanks' Folly.

Fairbanks was an interesting fellow. He served as Florida state senator and was editor of the *Florida Mirror* from 1879 to 1885, the same year he built the house. He authored *History of the University of the South*, *History of Florida*, and *The Spaniards in Florida*. He did other notable things, but there are far too many fascinating characters in Amelia's history to go in-depth on them all!

Lore has it that the house was dubbed Fairbanks Folly because he built it for his wife, who was not pleased with the end result. If true, one can only imagine how many options she must have had to hold such standards. The house is beautiful.

The Amelia Schoolhouse Inn

Schuyler designed this building to be used as an actual schoolhouse in 1886, when it was Schoolhouse Number 1. It served that function into the late 1990s, at which point it switched hands several times and served various purposes before being restored and put into operation as the Amelia Schoolhouse Inn in 2017. Visitors can stay there today.

St. Peter's Episcopal Church

Built in 1881 in the Gothic Revival style Schuyler was so famous for, St. Peter's Episcopal Church still stands as a beautiful testimony to his talents. It was rebuilt in 1892 after a devastating fire, but it was rebuilt almost exactly to its original specifications, losing only a spire.

Frank Lloyd Wright and the Blue Herron Inn

Yes, Fernandina has Frankl Lloyd Wright, too.

In 1904, the "greatest American architect of all time" designed the house currently serving as the Blue Herron Inn. It served as a clinic for an optometrist, among other things.

Chapter 15

Florida Cash and Fernandina's First Newspaper

Gregor MacGregor's reign as faux king of Amelia lasted only sixty-eight days, but it was enough time for him to order a printing press and make Florida's first-ever currency. It's an odd story solidly befitting MacGregor's court.

During the first week of MacGregor's occupation, he ordered a printing press to serve two primary purposes. The first was to produce a newspaper, and the second was to make currency notes that could be redeemed in the town customhouse. The first note was issued on August 19, 1817. MacGregor signed it himself, along with Joseph de Yrebarren, his secretary.

MacGregor tried using the "currency" to pay back the people that funded his doomed enterprise, but everyone recognized immediately that the notes were worthless. Ironically, they became worth more only after MacGregor's rule ended, with experts estimating the lone extant note at $20,000 as a collector's item back in 1980.

Chapter 16

Each of Us Must Play a Part

The People of Fernandina

Mary Mattair, Who Raised a Family in the Wilderness

Mary Mattair wasn't born into royalty. She wasn't a war hero or educator of orphans. She was just a woman of uncommonly resolute character, determination and courage—and for those qualities, she is one of Amelia Island's beloved daughters.

Mary and her husband, Lewis Zacharias Mattair, moved to St. Augustine while it was still under English rule (1763–83). There, Lewis died, leaving Mary alone with her son, Luis, eight, and daughter Maria, five. In the spring of 1783, with limited options before her, she requested land from the governor. Because she knew how to farm, the governor gave her five acres on the Amelia Island blufftop, at the spot where Fort San Carlos would one day stand.

The island was still mostly ruins due to Colonel Samuel Elbert's forces burning the town down in 1777. Mattair's little family took their first shelter in a warehouse that had been spared from the fires in order to provide shelter to Elbert's men. They lived on wild oranges and grapes and whatever else they could gather.

On September 3 that very year, only months after Mattair made her move, the Treaty of Paris put Florida back into Spain's hands. British citizens immediately began evacuating the area. Their overseers had banished Spanish citizens after taking over the island twenty years earlier, so they expected the same treatment in return. Mattair alone did not follow them, mostly because she had no means to do so. She and her children were barely scraping by at that point and had nowhere to go nor any resources to travel.

Spain surprisingly showed tremendous leniency. Mattair was allowed to stay in northern Florida for swearing loyalty alone and didn't have to convert to Catholicism. It was a rather amazing exception, as Catholicism basically defined the Spanish spirit at that time.

Spain needed Mattair's land because it offered the best strategic position from which to defend the island. In exchange, the Spanish offered her two hundred acres on the mainland opposite the island, which included a massive orange grove named Naranjal. The Spanish conducted the first census of their new rule in 1787 and listed Mary; her fifteen-year-old son, Luis; and her twelve-year-old daughter, Maria, as the only Amelia residents. It also noted they had two horses, three cows and nine pigs.

This was a time when nature was unforgiving and raiders and bandits still slinked through the surrounding countryside, yet this one woman successfully raised a family of three and grew her property to upward of eight hundred acres. She died in October 1790. Her land was split evenly between her children. Her daughter, Maria, went on to wed Domingo Fernández, a Spanish pilot, and build the Yellow Bluff Plantation.

Felipa the Witch

She left just enough of a footprint to let us know she was there but not so much that we know exactly who she was. When you have a name like Felipa the Witch, though, ambiguity is a positive. Imagination happily fills in holes that history leaves behind.

What we know is that there was a woman popularly known as Felipa the Witch. She was a freed Black woman who owned land in the Old Town area of Fernandina Beach. She owned multiple lots on Ladies Street, which is believed to have been a place of prostitution. The women mostly entertained soldiers from Fort San Carlos, the defensive post built to defend Amelia Island's residents.

Logs from the May 10, 1811, rezoning of Fernandina refer to her as Felipa "the Witch." The logs leave us a map and sparse documentation providing most of what we know about Felipa the Witch.

Felipa was known to make and sell charms and potions, including love potions. Considering the proximity of her business to Ladies Street, we can assume that "love potions" was a euphemism for aphrodisiacs, but that's not definitive. Love is always in demand, no matter the era or place.

Felipa sparked people's imaginations since day one. She inspired fictional characters, including one in *The Golden Isle* by Frank Slaughter, one of the major novelists of his era. In 1958, the Hemerocallis Garden Club held a show titled the Amelia Isle of Gold show, in honor of Slaughter's book.

We don't know much else about Felipa, which might be a good thing. With a name like that, reality would be hard-pressed to overshadow fantasy (unless your name is Jimmy Drummond).

THE SISTERS OF SAINT JOSEPH

One cluster of tombstones in Bosque Bello consists of simple stones with just a name and a cross on them. They mark the resting places of the Sisters of St. Joseph. Their fascinating story more than warrants its own section.

The Sisters of St. Joseph is a Roman Catholic order founded in 1650 in France. Some Sisters moved to St. Augustine in 1866 to educate African Americans in the aftermath of the Civil War. They taught children and adults alike.

Some of the Sisters quickly migrated to Fernandina to set up schools and shelters. They weren't paid for their work and had to sell crafts and give lessons in art, music and the French language to make ends meet. Their discipline and work ethic were considerable.

The Sisters acted as nurses when yellow fever broke out in 1877. Amelia experienced multiple yellow fever outbreaks, but 1877 was the worst. Around 1,100 people got sick—so many that the city practically came to a standstill. The Sisters responded. As Fernandina residents streamed out of the city for safer climes, the Sisters streamed in. They nursed the sick, helped bury the dead and prayed and cared for everyone.

Mother Marie Célenie Joubert and Sister Marie de Sales Kennedy were two Sisters among the ninety-four Amelia residents who died from the fever. Kennedy was twenty-six years old, and Joubert was thirty-three. Originally buried in the Fernandez Reserve Burial Grounds, they were exhumed and moved to Bosque Bello years later. Regional lore claims that the undertaker encountered an overwhelming smell of roses on unearthing them and that he opened the caskets to find that neither woman had decomposed at all.

The Sisters were back on duty in 1818 when yellow fever broke out again and killed fifty-four Fernandina residents. In 1956, Sister Anna Josephine Perbet became the last of the Sisters to rest in Bosque Bello. She died at ninety-four, having lived out the last sixty-five years of her life in Fernandina, far from her birthplace in Tanse, France.

The Sisters of St. Joseph still serve in Florida. They have schools in Jacksonville, St. Augustine and Miami.

Amelia Island Museum of History flyer promoting posthumous exhibit on Mayor Charles Albert. *Amelia Island Museum of History.*

Mayor Charles Albert

Charles Albert was the first Black mayor of Fernandina Beach. That fact alone deserves mention here in a book about a place that experienced so much racial strife in its past.

Albert passed away in January 2021 at the age of eighty-eight. Before becoming the mayor in 1978, he spent eighteen years on the city commission. Before that, he was a teacher. He was a man always concerned with civic duty and one who left a positive mark (and happy memories) on his home.

Amos Latham: The First Lighthouse Keeper

The first lightkeeper on Amelia Island was Amos Latham. He started the job in 1829, when the lighthouse still stood on Cumberland Island, and traveled with the structure when it went to Amelia.

Latham was born in Groton, Connecticut, to Jasper and Deborah Latham on July 19, 1759. In May 1777, at the age of sixteen, he joined the Continental army and climbed to the rank of corporal in the First Connecticut regiment. He was there at the brutal 1777–78 wintering at Valley Forge, Pennsylvania. For that season, badly equipped and underfed men, many of whom didn't even have shoes, suffered through rampant disease outbreaks that killed roughly two thousand soldiers.

Yet when it was done, the Valley Forge soldiers continued fighting the war, including the Battle of Monmouth. Many men died on both sides, but Latham again survived, having experienced an eternity's worth of challenge, hardship and horror—all before the age of eighteen.

Latham didn't get out of Monmouth unscathed. He sat out the war while healing a wounded leg. He wanted to go right back to duty after he recovered, but his injury prevented him. So Latham found his way back into service by becoming a marine in the Continental navy.

Latham spent October 1778 to August 1781 on a frigate named the USS *Confederacy*. In 1782, he became a prisoner of war when two British warships overtook the *Confederacy* as it headed home from the West Indies full of military supplies and leading thirty-seven merchantmen.

The Continentals were near the Delaware Capes when he fell prisoner. He wound up in a prison ship named *Jersey* and stayed there until being released into Charleston, South Carolina. After that, Latham bounced around from Pennsylvania to Virginia and, finally, to Georgia, where he was granted two hundred acres of land near the Satilla River.

Latham took the job of lightkeeper in 1829 and performed it until his death in 1842. He was buried near the lighthouse, with his wife, Jane (who died in 1840), before both were moved to Bosque Bello. They had produced two children, Jane Maria Latham and George Washington Avery Latham. Despite a life of adventure in war, Amos reached the ripe old age of eighty-two.

If you visit Amos in Bosque Bello, you'll see that his tombstone claims his birth date was April 18, 1759, which contradicts the birth date provided above. Well, friends, the error is not to be laid at the feet of your author. The makers of the tombstone used the date Amos provided in his pension application. Amos himself had gotten his birthday wrong. His descendant, Sallie McNeil, who wrote an extensive genealogy of Amos, has suggested that maybe his mind had grown "fuzzy" in older age.

Like so many other things about Amelia Island, we'll never know the answer for sure.

Chapter 17

Gilberto Shrimping Weed Boat of 1977

Thanksgiving Day, 1977: A shrimp boat barrels over early morning waters. Three men squat inside, squinting through heavy fog. The men jostle about like loose vegetables in a grocery basket as a jolt shoots through the craft. The ship stops, stuck, run aground on Amelia Island.

The men react differently than we expect. Rather than running for assistance or laughing good-naturedly at the mishap, they set their cargo on fire. Quickly, the overwhelming smell of marijuana hits the air. Amelia Islanders come running.

The boat was named the *Gilberto*, and the men were Cuban Americans Mariono C. Iglesias, Lorenzo I. Aros and Pedro Pacheco. The trio would soon be known as the Gilberto Three. They'd go down in infamy for the biggest, most comical drug bust in Fernandina history.

The events leading up to the beaching are unclear. Police suspect that the three men loaded cargo off a larger ship in deeper water, but no one could prove that. However they got the stuff, the men were transporting more than a ton of marijuana when they got twisted around in morning fog and ran aground.

The three had been in a Cuban prison just the summer before. They'd been out retrieving lobster traps (at least that was their story) when a Cuban gunboat ordered them ashore. Authorities found something on the boat that caused them to imprison the men for thirty days, after which point the trio headed back to the States. It's possible they were released due to pressure

Vintage photograph of authorities at the burning Gilberto weed boat. *Amelia Island Museum of History.*

from a timely visit to Cuba by Senator Frank Church, who of course had no idea that just a year later, the men would be busted in America.

As the fire raged on and news of the incident spread, people began rushing to the beach, some just to witness the spectacle and others to pocket some chunks that were scattered across the sands. The police tried to manage the curious crowd while also putting out the fire. Witnesses remember it as a comical scene. Despite the distractions, police were able to retrieve twenty-seven bales before the boat exploded.

Much of the *Gilberto*'s cargo burned up, but police were able to put enough together to charge the men with possession and intent to distribute forty-eight thousand pounds (twenty-four tons) of marijuana. So much of it had been scattered that police raked it into heaps.

The police kept some of the cargo for evidence and disposed of the rest in a wood mill. No one is sure how much wound up in the hands of the scavenging public.

A piece published earlier that month in the Fernandina Beach *News-Leader* was titled "Marijuana: Smoked by All Kinds in Nassau County." It was part of a series on marijuana consumption and how all levels of society were doing it.

Vintage photograph of the burned Gilberto weed boat. *Amelia Island Museum of History.*

A resident named Paul Rider made commemorative shirts reading, "Thanksgiving 1977—Fernandina Beach, Florida—25 tons." The defendants themselves asked for the shirts, and Rider obliged. During the fortieth anniversary of the event in 2017, Pajamadave Voorhees of PJD's Beer & Wine Garden sold replicas.

A notable Fernandina Beach band is named Gilberto '77.

DIAMANTE

Looking back with 2020s eyes, many find the Gilberto weed boat humorous. Attitudes tend to change when it comes hard drugs, but this tale of mysterious cocaine is interesting.

On November 7, 2019, two women strolling along Fernandina Beach came across a tightly wrapped package. On the outside of the package, written in marker, was the word DIAMANTE, in all capital letters. The women took the package to police, who quickly identified it as a kilo of cocaine.

What makes the story interesting is that the discovery was only a small part of an international phenomenon that's still being unraveled as of this writing. Kilos of cocaine marked DIAMANTE have not only turned up in much greater quantities on Florida beaches such as Melbourne and Cocoa Beach but also across the pond in France. Massive amounts of the stuff have been turned over to the authorities. We can only guess how much more is out there, floating in the ocean or in the private possession of finders who chose to be keepers.

Sorry for the Weight

Fernandina Beach is known for its picturesque beauty, quaint downtown and mellow pace. Yet it, too, has its shadows.

In June 2015, police executed Operation Sorry for the Weight, a major undercover campaign aimed at a Fernandina Beach drug network. The bust led to the arrest of twenty-five men and women. The drugs confiscated were everything from marijuana to crack cocaine, methamphetamine and Xanax.

Chapter 18

Just A-Passing Through

Stories of Amelia's Notable Visitors

Zora Neale Hurston Married in Fernandina

Zora Neale Hurston is one of the true giants of American literature. Her novel *Their Eyes Were Watching God* and her short stories and essays are still taught in high school and university programs around the country. She was also an important folklorist and anthropologist—in short, a remarkable woman by any measure.

Hurston was born in 1891 in Notasulga, Alabama. She married three times. Her second husband was Albert Price, grandson of Alfred W. Price, for whom Price Street in American Beach is named. They married on June 27, 1939, in Fernandina Beach. Price was considerably younger than Zora, being twenty-three to her thirty-eight, and the marriage fell apart in less than a year.

Hurston was known to visit American Beach, but we have frustratingly (for fans of Zora, anyway) little information on the details.

Harriet Tubman in Fernandina

Imagine this: Harriet Tubman, hero of the Underground Railroad, slipping quietly through the streets of Fernandina Beach and gathering intelligence for war. Sounds outlandish, but it might have happened.

Tubman was one of the United States' most notable abolitionists, a truly towering figure whose life sounds more like that of a folk hero than a real flesh-and-blood person. Her work liberating slaves has understandably overshadowed her other feats, including being the first woman to lead a U.S. military expedition. Tubman was a Union spy in the Civil War. She traveled through the South gathering intelligence from slaves behind Confederate lines.

What's less clear is if Tubman performed that function in Fernandina.

What we know is that the Union commander of Amelia Island reached out to Tubman during a dysentery outbreak among the soldiers in 1863. She'd established a solid reputation as a nurse and healer. Yet considering that we know she performed other clandestine duties, it's not at all unreasonable to surmise that she was performing some cloak-and-dagger activities undercover as a nurse.

Unfortunately, we may never know for sure. Tubman's exploits in Amelia were thinly recorded, and we have only a couple scraps of information to work from. Still, she's big enough that even the possibility of her presence deserves a mention.

BANDIT MCGIRT

Daniel McGirt is one of Florida's most notable outlaws. A South Carolina native born sometime in 1750, McGirt made a name for himself during the Revolutionary War. Having been a trapper and hunter, he served effectively as a scout in the Continental army before switching over to the British Loyalists.

McGirt terrorized the southern Georgia and northern Florida landscape through the late 1700s. With his gang, he robbed, raped and murdered, building a reputation for such remorseless violence that Native tribes couldn't be persuaded to move against him. He entered the Amelia saga in 1783, after Spain retook the island and gave English citizens eighteen months to leave. The resulting flights created a chaotic situation that was ripe for McGirt and his crew to take advantage of.

Eventually Governor Zéspedes organized a posse that was able to successfully arrest the ever-dangerous McGirt crew. They were imprisoned in St. Augustine before being moved to Havana in 1785. McGirt was banished from all Spanish territories. He jumped onboard a ship and escaped to East Florida (then a Spanish territory) before being caught and sent to the Bahamas. His fate is a bit hazy, but evidence suggests that he

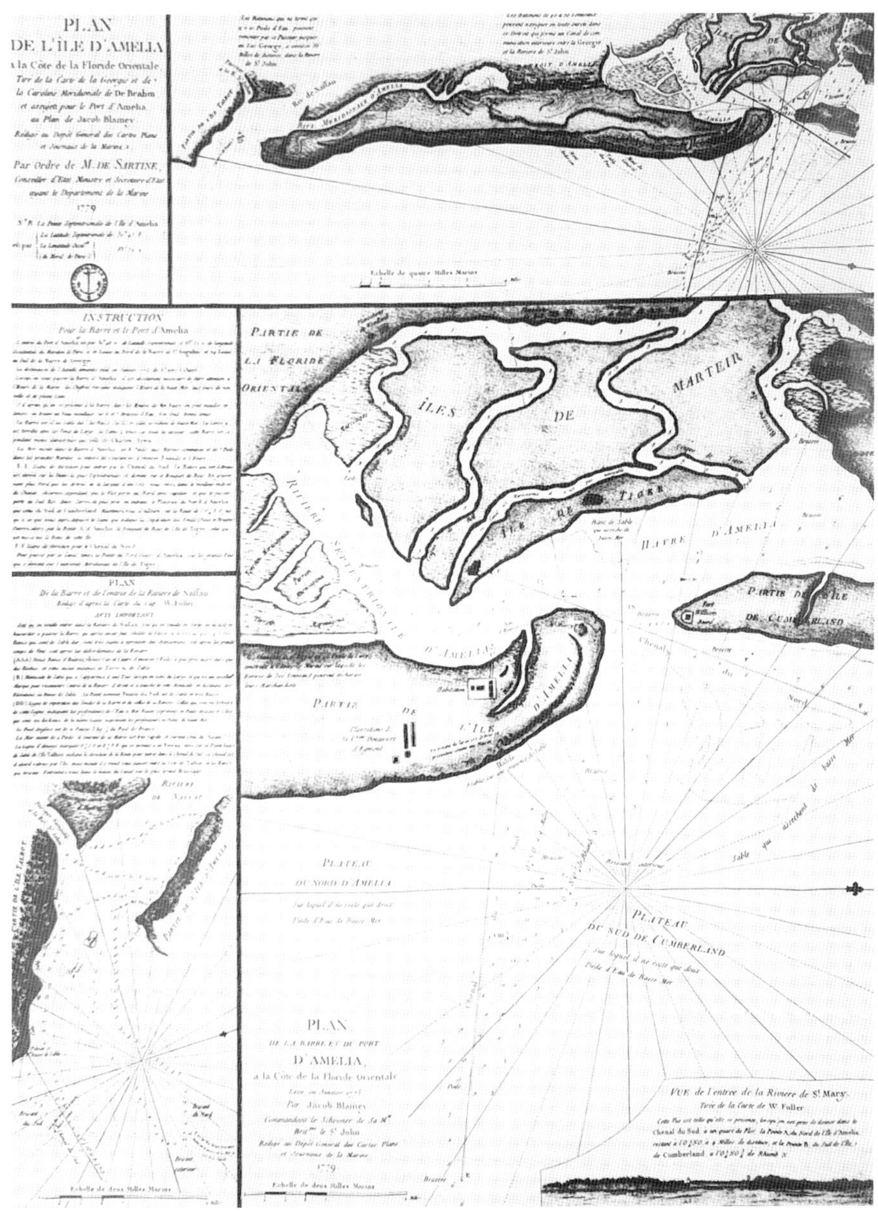

A 1779 French map of Amelia Island. *Amelia Island Museum of History.*

was able to use his considerable political connections to live out his final years in peace in Georgia.

Bibliography

Amelia Island Museum of History. Online Collections Database. https://ameliaisland.pastperfectonline.com/.

———. Veterans History Project. https://ameliamuseum.org/veteran-history-project/

Amelia Island Museum of History and the University of Florida Center for Landscape Conservation Planning. "The History of Fernandina's Waterfront." ArcGIS: Story Maps. https://storymaps.arcgis.com/stories/f640318c09144c3d91b84aff48768902.

Amelia Research and Recovery. "The Amelia Island Project." https://ameliaresearch.com/amelia-island.

Arsenault, Kathleen Hardee. "Looking for Treasure on Amelia Island." *Fernandina Observer*, April 12, 2021. https://fernandinaobserver.com/featured-story/looking-for-treasure-on-amelia-island/.

Boucher, Diane. "Mayhem and Murder in the East Florida Frontier 1783 to 1789." *Florida Historical Quarterly* 93, no. 3 (2015): 446–71. http://www.jstor.org/stable/43487697.

Bowman, Charles H. "Vicente Pazos, Agent for the Amelia Island Filibusters, 1818." *Florida Historical Quarterly* 53, no. 4 (1975): 428–42. http://www.jstor.org/stable/30150298.

———. "Vicente Pazos and the Amelia Island Affair, 1817." *Florida Historical Quarterly* 53, no. 3 (1975): 273–95. http://www.jstor.org/stable/30145960.

Chandler, Billy Jaynes. "Harmon Murray: Black Desperado in Late Nineteenth-Century Florida." *Florida Historical Quarterly* 73, no. 2 (1994): 184–99. http://www.jstor.org/stable/30148759.

Chicago Tribune. "Merrick Jackson Hanged at Fernandina, Fla., for the Murder of a Colored Man." August 5, 1882.

City of Fernandina Beach. "Jimmy Drummond." In "Stories from Bosque Bello." https://fbfl.us/DocumentCenter/View/17372/Stories-from-Bosque-Bello---Jimmy-Drummond?bidId=.

Dabney, Lancaster E. "Louis Aury: The First Governor of Texas under the Mexican Republic." *Southwestern Historical Quarterly* 42, no. 2 (1938): 108–16. http://www.jstor.org/stable/30235814.

Daniels, Jason. "Shipwrecked in the Atlantic World: Reevaluating Jonathan Dickinson's Interactions with Native Peoples along Florida's Southeastern Coast." *Florida Historical Quarterly* 91, no. 4 (2013): 451–90. http://www.jstor.org/stable/43487529.

Davis, T. Frederick. "Florida Historical Material in Niles' Register." *Florida Historical Quarterly* 19, no. 2 (1940): 155–62. http://www.jstor.org/stable/30138365.

———. "MacGregor's Invasion of Florida, 1817." *Florida Historical Society Quarterly* 7, no. 1 (1928): 2–71. http://www.jstor.org/stable/30150809.

Edenfield, Gray. *Amelia Island: Birthplace of the Modern Shrimping Industry*. Stroud, England: Fonthill Media, 2015.

Fannin, John F. "The Jacksonville Mutiny of 1865." *Florida Historical Quarterly* 88, no. 3 (2010): 368–96. http://www.jstor.org/stable/20700299.

Fishman, Laura. "Old World Images Encounter New World Reality: Rene Laudonniere and the Timucuans of Florida." *Sixteenth Century Journal* 26, no. 3 (1995): 547–59. https://doi.org/10.2307/2543138.

Florida Mirror. "Hanged by the Neck: Merrick Jackson Expiates His Crime Upon the Gallows." August 5, 1882.

Florida Times-Union. "Pirate Gold Believed to Be Buried on Amelia Island Is Lure for Treasure Hunters." November 25, 1935.

Florida State Parks. "The History of Yellow Bluff." https://www.floridastateparks.org/learn/history-yellow-bluff.

Foster, Sarah Whitmer, and John T. Foster. "Chloe Merrick Reed: Freedom's First Lady." *Florida Historical Quarterly* 71, no. 3 (1993): 279–99. http://www.jstor.org/stable/30148214.

Gorman, M. Adele Francis. "Jean Ribault's Colonies in Florida." *Florida Historical Quarterly* 44, no. 1/2 (1965): 51–66. http://www.jstor.org/stable/30147726.

Jaccard, D.L. *The Historic Splendor of Amelia Island*. Fernandina Beach, FL: Larus Books. 1997.

Jensen, S.R. *Amelia Island Book of Secrets*. Bloomington, IN: AuthorHouse, 2021.

Lowe, Richard G. "American Seizure of Amelia Island." *Florida Historical Quarterly* 45, no. 1 (1966): 18–30. http://www.jstor.org/stable/30145698.

Lyon, Eugene. *The Enterprise of Florida: Pedro Menéndez de Aviles and the Spanish Conquest of 1565–1568*. Gainesville: University Presses of Florida, 1929.

Mackie, Julie. "Brick of Cocaine Found on Beach." SearchAmelia.com. https://www.searchamelia.com/brick-of-cocaine-found-on-beach.

Martin, Susan. "The Fernandez Reserve." Amelia Island Museum of History, April 25, 2023. https://ameliamuseum.org/the-fernandina-reserve/.

Meadows, A.L. *The Amelia Island Travel Guide*. Columbia, SC: self-published, 2022.

Menéndez de Avilés, Pedro. "Letter to King Philip II." Early Visions of Florida. https://earlyfloridalit.net/pedro-menendez-de-aviles-letter-to-king-philip-ii/.

Miami Herald. "Crewmen Held on Drug Charges." November 26, 1977. https://www.newspapers.com/image/627761128.

———. "3 Fishermen Were 'Wanted,' Cuba Says." July 9, 1997. https://www.newspapers.com/image/623248296/.

Monroe, James. "Message from the President of the United States, to both Houses of Congress, at the Commencement of the First Session of the Fifteenth Congress." Washington, D.C.: Edward de Krafft, 1817. Available at https://www.govinfo.gov/content/pkg/SERIALSET-00002_00_00-001-0001-0000/pdf/SERIALSET-00002_00_00-001-0001-0000.pdf.

Moore, Roger, and Kurtz, Ron. *Amelia Island and Fernandina Beach*. Amelia Island, FL: Photographs Naturally, 2008.

News-Leader (Fernandina Beach, FL). "Local Shrimping Declared Disaster." September 13, 1978. https://original-ufdc.uflib.ufl.edu/UF00079912/01005.

Nicklas, Steve. "Amelia Island Treasure Hunters: In Search of the *San Miguel*: Buried Treasure Worth $2 Billion." Amelia Island Living, April 2013. https://ameliaislandliving.com/fernandinabeach/2013/04/amelia-island-treasure-hunters-in-search-of-the-san-miguel-buried-treasure-worth-2-billion/.

Palm Beach Post. "Palm Beachers to Seek Captain Kidd's Treasure." November 25, 1935. https://www.newspapers.com/image/134064600/.

"The Patriot War, a Contemporaneous Letter." *Florida Historical Society Quarterly* 5, no. 3 (1927): 162–67. http://www.jstor.org/stable/30150752.

Phelts, Marsha Dean. *An American Beach for African Americans*. Gainesville: University Press of Florida, 1997.

Salis, Ivan. "A Real Pirates Treasure Tale * Luis Aury Of Amelia Island—($60,000) In 1817 Money." Treasure.net, August 29, 2012. https://www.treasurenet.com/threads/a-real-pirates-treasure-tale-luis-aury-of-amelia-island-60-000-in-1817-money.310010/.

Stagg, J.C.A. Review of *Revolutionizing East Florida, Mobile, and Pensacola in 1812*, by George Mathews and John McKee. *Florida Historical Quarterly* 85, no. 3 (2007): 269–96. http://www.jstor.org/stable/30150062.

Vickery, Paul S. "Bartolomé de las Casas: Prophet of the New World." *Mediterranean Studies* 9 (2000): 89–102. http://www.jstor.org/stable/41166913.

Ward, Christopher. "The Commerce of East Florida during the Embargo, 1806-1812: The Role of Amelia Island." *Florida Historical Quarterly* 68, no. 2 (1989): 160–79. http://www.jstor.org/stable/30148064.

Weekly Floridian. "A Terrible Tragedy." February 12, 1884. https://www.newspapers.com/image/893535730.

Wyllys, Rufus Kay. "The Filibusters of Amelia Island." *Georgia Historical Quarterly* 12, no. 4 (1928): 297–325. http://www.jstor.org/stable/40575973.

About the Author

Jeff Suwak has been a professional writer and editor for over two decades, with experience ranging from fiction to music journalism to technical communication and earth sciences. He moved to north Florida in 2022 and fell in love with its landscape, its people and its history. He is also a ghostwriter and always interested in hearing about new projects at jeffsuwak@gmail.com.